LAW ON THE ELECTRONIC FRONTIER WITHDRAWN

THE DAVID HUME INSTITUTE

Hume Papers on Public Policy
Volume 2 No 4 Winter 1994

LAW ON THE ELECTRONIC FRONTIER

Ian J Lloyd and Moira Simpson

EDINBURGH UNIVERSITY PRESS

© David Hume Institute 1994

Edinburgh University Press
22 George Square, Edinburgh

Typeset in Times New Roman by ROM-Data Corporation Ltd.,
Falmouth, Cornwall and printed and bound in Great Britain by
Page Bros. Limited, Norwich

A CIP record for this book is available from the
British Library

ISBN 0 7486 0594 0

Contents

Contributors

Dr Ian J Lloyd is Reader in Law and Co-Director of the Centre for Law, Computers and Technology; **Moira Simpson** Lecturer in Legal Informatics; both in the Law School, University of Strathclyde.

Foreword

With this issue of *Hume Papers on Public Policy* the reader is taken into cyberspace and the tangles of the *Internet*, a universe traversed by the "information super highway", populated by hackers, and filled with phracking, packet sniffing, and magic cookies. It is a universe which Ian Lloyd and Moira Simpson compare to the traditional Wild West of the cowboy movie, with images of the frontier, outlaws and dangerous natives; the question which they address is the function of the sheriff, if he can be found. At first sight it may all seem rather a long way from the usual austere concerns of The David Hume Institute. Yet the Information Technology Revolution which has produced all these things is already influencing our world as profoundly as the Industrial Revolution did the world of David Hume and Adam Smith, and it behoves us to consider what some of the implications of this transformation may be.

Law on the Electronic Frontier is primarily concerned with the response of law. Ian Lloyd and Moira Simpson demonstrate in vivid fashion how traditional legal concepts such as property and ownership are struggling to keep in step with the possibilities opened up by the new and still-developing technology. Indeed the very basis of law as a series of nationally determined jurisdictions is undermined by the ease with which information and ideas may now flow across frontiers. But further, as the authors point out, this easy transfer also has the potential to threaten the privacy and perhaps even the freedom of the individual, inasmuch as decisions about individuals are now frequently made, not on the basis of any personal knowledge or assessment, but upon previously recorded information to which the decision-maker alone has access. While this may seem to remove some of the threat of bias or prejudice or delay in decision-making, accountability, flexibility and responsiveness to particular circumstances may be lost. There is a real need, the authors argue, to introduce a more appropriate framework of regulation than at present exists, and to do so upon a supra-national footing. The opportunities are exciting but the threat no less real.

The David Hume Institute must as usual disclaim any commitment to the view of its authors, but *Law on the Electronic Frontier* may be recommended as both a survey of the current state of the Information Technology Revolution and as a contribution to the debate over the best framework of law and regulation with which to facilitate and control its effects.

Hector L MacQueen
Executive Director
The David Hume Institute

Introduction

What's Special About the Computer?

In St Matthew's Gospel we are told how five loaves and two fishes provided a meal for five thousand (Chapter 14 Verse 17). It is further recounted how, when everyone had eaten their fill, the remaining scraps filled 12 baskets. The inference must be that more food was left at the end of the meal than had been in existence at the beginning. In the physical world, such an occurrence can only be described as miraculous. Resources are finite and generally, to use the colloquialism, cake cannot be both held and eaten. A second aspect of the miracle also deserves attention from a legal perspective. If I possess food, its acquisition by a third party will result in the loss of my possession. The rights of a property owner can be secured adequately only by conferring some element of exclusivity. The owner of a car (or a loaf of bread) is - subject to the inevitable exceptions - free to use or dispose of the object in any manner thought fit. Civil or criminal sanctions may be imposed against anyone who interferes with the owner's rights.

What is miraculous in the corporeal field is commonplace in the incorporeal. Ideas are infinite and the tendency of the law has been to deny that rights of ownership can apply to these. As was said by Thomas Jefferson, one of the framers of the United States' constitution:

> If nature has made any one thing less susceptible than all others of exclusive property, it is that action of the thinking power called an idea, which an individual may exclusively possess as long as he keeps it to himself; but the moment it is divulged, it forces itself into the possession of everyone, and the receiver cannot dispossess himself of it. ... He who receives an idea from me, receives instructions himself without lessening mine; as he who lights his taper at mine, receives light without darkening me. That ideas should be spread from one to another over the globe, for the moral and mutual instructions of man, and improvement of his condition, seems to have been peculiarly and designed by nature ...

Many of the issues involved and the framework of the legal response predate the computer. In the 18th and 19th centuries, the industrial revolution transformed the physical world. Control of natural resources such as coal or iron ore, coupled with that of the communications infrastructure required for their transportation, became the key to wealth and power and resulted in a massive increase in their exploitation. The plans of those who wished to build and operate railroads, however, frequently conflicted with the wishes of those who owned the land over or adjacent to which the metal monsters were intended to travel. These disputes formed the basis for many of the landmark parliamentary battles of the Railway Age. In the agricultural field, the enclosure of land marked a move from common ownership to private or individual ownership. Anyone familiar with the movies will recognise a similar phenomenon in the Wild West where the arrival of the wagon trains brought waves of settlers intent on claiming ownership of land hitherto not recognised as being owned by anyone (except the Indians who obviously did not count).

The Wild West analogy furnishes an appropriate theme for the present work. Its basic thesis asserts that we are living on a new, electronic, frontier. The question to be addressed concerns the manner in which the law should be applied to the new forms of behaviour resulting from the invention and application of the computer. One of the more notorious phenomena of the computer age has been that of computer hacking. The nature and legal implications of this will be discussed in detail in chapter three. In terms of the present analogy the computer hacker may be seen as a modern equivalent of the gunslinger. Here discussion is only partly concerned with the question whether conduct is prohibited by the law. Of greater significance are questions as to the adequacy of law enforcement and the obtaining and presentation before a court of the evidence necessary to secure a conviction. In other areas, direct marketeers and the controllers of data bases may be equated with the railroad barons and the mining undertakings whose insatiable thirst for resources threatened the interests of other landowners located downstream from their activities. The system of riparian rights in respect of access to and use of water is adequate for regulating the activities of private parties, less so when water becomes an industrial resource. Here the issue is the more significant one whether existing legal models are suitable for the new age. When a car or a domestic appliance breaks down, its owner is faced with the choice whether to seek to have it repaired or to replace it with a new model. A similar dilemma faces today's law makers. In a number of significant areas, the introduction of information technology is exposing limitations in existing legal provisions. The question whether the response should involve repair or replacement is of critical importance.

It is difficult to identify a single area of law or of life which is not at least potentially affected by information technology. This work will consider four key topics; the impact of computerised record keeping practices upon individual privacy, the extent to which computer related conduct might incur sanctions under the criminal law, the application of the copyright system to computer software and, finally, the nature and extent of the liabilities which may be incurred in the event that the improper operation of software results in some form of injury or damage.

Chapter One

Crime and the Computer

Introduction

Articles, books and even Hollywood movies have explored the world of the computer hacker. Whether regarded as a modern day equivalent of Robin Hood or of Atilla the Hun, the criminal consequences of computer-related conduct increasingly constitute the subject of both popular and legal debate.

In many instances, the fact of a computer's involvement in some scheme of criminal conduct raises no novel legal issues. Where the computer is involved in some scheme of fraud, there is little doubt that some form of theft-related offence will be committed at the time when the perpetrator acquires possession of the funds in question. There may be dispute when an offence is committed. Given the speed and potential scale of electronic fund transfers - one oft-quoted estimate has it that the United Kingdom's currency reserves could be transferred abroad in 15 minutes - this is a matter of considerable practical significance, not least in that there may be a jurisdictional issue where the proceeds of a fraud are realised outwith the United Kingdom (see *R v Thompson* [1984] 3 All ER 565 concerning the attempt to realise in England the proceeds of a computer fraud perpetrated on a bank in Kuwait). The focus of the present work will be on those areas where the question whether conduct is criminal is open to doubt. As with data protection, concerns at the adequacy of existing legal provisions has led to the enactment of computer specific legislation, in this case in the form of the Computer Misuse Act 1990. Again, therefore, a major element of the work must involve consideration how effective this legislation is likely to prove as a response to the challenges facing the law.

What is a 'hacker'?

> Articles written about "hackers" and the "computer underground" are invariably senseless, inaccurate, and sensationalistic. The writers of said articles have a strong preconceived notion, every "fact" they collect either reinforces that notion, is twisted to reinforce that notion, or is discarded, and they pass the resulting tripe onto readers who don't know enough about the subject to do anything but believe the report ((Kevin Andrew Buhr) alt. hackers).

The media depiction of a hacker tends to be that of a male teenager in a greasy T-shirt and torn jeans who spends 27 hours slumped over a terminal, eyes gazing fixedly at the green glow of the VDU monitor. Banks, military installations, universities, companies and financial institutions fall before his relentless onslaught. Nowhere is safe, no one can keep him out, no one knows of the scale of the threat, the silent deadly menace that stalks the networks. A juvenile prodigy who programmed from the age of three, the hacker possesses boundless, unsurpassable knowledge of every operating system and is endowed with a remarkable natural talent for programming. Fluent in all languages, he can write special programs to overcome all obstacles and can cover his electronic traces to leave no sign of intrusion. The hacker has no friends, likes heavy metal music, has never had a girlfriend and gains all sense of self-worth through pounding the keyboards and controlling the world's networks.

Possibly this is itself a stereotype of a media stereotype and is over simplistic but such imagery is widely scattered throughout much 'hacker' reporting. The UK hacker, Neil Woods, who was arrested and charged under the Computer Misuse Act in 1991, although admitting to having hacked into many computers, complained that the mere mention of the word 'hacking' appeared to generate an atmosphere of exaggerated fear and hysteria about what hackers were capable of doing:

> There were a lot of incredible stories in the press, such as we delayed the gulf war because we gained access to a met.office computer, and they thought we were a foreign power - the computer was supposedly supplying forecasts for the gulf area at the time ... don't believe most of what you read about us, a lot of it is factually incorrect, from our ages up to what we were alleged to have hacked. I don't blame journalists for some of it though, as there was a lot of garbage said in court (e-mail correspondence from Neil Woods).

Genuine uncertainty about what a hacker is provokes much of this kind of reaction. Many people assume that hackers are necessarily possessed of strange and sinister talents which enable them to gain free access to the world's computers and that often their motives are malicious and their activities dangerous. In the Net News (a term for the many and varied electronic discussion groups which are available on the Internet) group, *Alt.Hackers*, Jef Poskanzer regularly warns readers what the news group is really all about.

> What's a hacker? This is kind of like asking a Zen Buddhist "What is Zen?", or asking Louis Armstrong "What is jazz?" ...There was a period in the 80s when the media used "hacker" to mean someone who breaks into computer systems. They were using the word incorrectly. Some people who came of age during that period believed the media's incorrect definition, applied it to themselves, and now think they are some sort of glorious outlaw hacker. These people are sadly misguided. Perhaps someday they will figure out what hacking is really about. Perhaps reading this news group will help ...

Hacking is a generic expression in the computing world and can be applied in many contexts. The *New Hacker's Dictionary* compiled by Eric S Raymond (1993) defines hacking in various ways

1. A person who enjoys exploring the details of programmable systems and how to stretch their capabilities, as opposed to most users, who prefer to learn only the minimum necessary.
2. One who programs enthusiastically (even obsessively)...
3. A person good at programming quickly
4. An expert in a particular language or operating system, i.e. a UNIX®[1] hacker
5. One who enjoys the intellectual challenge of overcoming or circumventing limitations
6. A malicious meddler who tries to discover sensitive information by poking around

Generally speaking, at least in strictly computing terms, a hack is a quick fix or clever solution to a restriction. A 'hack' is a temporary if ingenious fix or 'make do' rather than an attack on a system. Tricking a dumb machine into performing an unintended task is the predominant characteristic of a 'hack'; even well-known simple tricks such as sticking sellotape over pre-recorded tapes to enable reuse as a 'blank' tape can be described as 'hacks'.

The History of 'Hacking'

Hacking, as most people are dimly aware, predates the computing age. It began in the golden days of phone phreaking in which the telecommunications system of America was subjected to constant misuse by those seeking free calls and unpaid for services. The basic technique was to simulate valid system sounds by other means (including a whistle given away free in breakfast cereal which it was discovered could emit a high pitched shriek exactly like that of a tone which gave full operator's privileges). The aims of phone phreaking may seem straightforward - avoidance of payment was a major incentive; however even back in those days, motives other than purely financial could be detected. 'Phreakers' enjoyed the thrill of the game, the mastery over the machine, outwitting 'the system' and generally asserting intellectual superiority.

Computer 'hacking' retains many of these principles and was a natural progression from 'phreaking' phones, as networked computers even today are simply computers hooked up via telecommunication lines whether by traditional analogue telephone lines, the latest ISDN lines or by satellite. The 'hacker' Net News group, alt.2600, which continues its existence on the *Internet*, takes its name from the 2600 hertz that enabled phone phreaks to access the phone system.

Phrack: The Hacking Trade Magazine

Phrack is an electronic magazine which attempts to be an unofficial trade magazine for 'hackers'/'crackers'. Founded in the early 1980s, it has enjoyed a colourful and eventful history and continues in publication today, although not in the same editorial hands. The journal shows all the hallmarks of a juvenile and amateurish enterprise and lacks any coherent structure. It consists of telecommunications information (Phrack = Phreaking/Hacking) and detailed information on operating systems security loopholes (they do not claim to be doing this to benefit system owners!). Issues of *Phrack* which appeared in the 1980s have a strong 'dark side cracking' edge to them in their descriptions of system breaking and the abuse of the telecommunications system. In its 1990s incarnation, it has adopted a slightly more restrained tone and could perhaps pass as a system security discussion group. The editors assert that they have always avoided publishing anything of an overtly illegal nature.

Members of the *Phrack* editorial board were at one time associated with the 'Legion of Doom' , a hacker group which operated in the United States in the late 1980s. The group's wide-ranging activities included diversion of telephone networks, copying proprietary information from companies and distributing 'hacking' tutorials. In 1990, two 'Legion of Doom' members were prosecuted under the American Wire Fraud and Computer Fraud and Abuse Statutes for their alleged misappropriation of confidential information relating to the operation of the emergency 911 telephone service. During the trial, the semantics of the term 'hacking' emerged as an issue. One 'Legion of Doom' member objected to being described in court as a 'hacker' as he felt such a term was 'unnecessary and prejudicial' (*United States v Riggs* 739 F Supp 414 (1990)). The court however found that such a term was acceptable to describe persons who gain unauthorised access to computers. Reference was made to Webster's II New Riverside University Dictionary which defines a hacker as "Slang. One who gains unauthorised, usually non-fraudulent access to another's computer system", with the term being taken generally to mean both those who gain unauthorised access and those who enjoy investigating computer operating systems.

Dark Side Hackers or Crackers

Such terms are often used to describe the 'bad' hacker, although the use of 'Star Wars' terminology might be thought still to glamorise and romanticise their activities. The use of such alternative descriptions represents an attempt by non-malicious hackers to distance themselves from the criminal activities of certain notorious hacking/cracking rings. A previous demarcation had attempted to establish use of the term 'worm' to describe the benign sister of the 'virus' (a worm was supposed to be a harmless self-replicating program). However this linguistic readjustment failed spectacularly when Robert Morris' famous *Internet* worm created havoc in 1988. The fact that Morris' worm had started life as an apparently innocent creature and had been intended only to demonstrate programming ability, and in the well worn hacker phrase, 'to expose security problems', highlights the difficulties inherent in attempting to distinguish between 'good' and 'bad' 'hackers'.

In some cases, the 'hacker'/'cracker' may not be a programming genius or 'Whizz Kid' but may rather have characteristics in common with that other predominantly male pursuit[2] – trainspotting. This type of 'hacker'/'cracker' accumulates vast quantities of information, which in itself may be unimportant but which can be manipulated to form a whole, which if not larger than the sum of its parts, at least gives its possessor the knowledge necessary to begin 'tweaking' the system. All manner of detail concerning the minutiae of operating systems is collected with amateurish enthusiasm. Just as the train spotter through exhaustive tabulation of train times may work out an optimum route to avoid ticket collectors, such a hacker may work out a 'route' from unauthorised logger on to root access. Some hacks may be very simple. A recent discussion on the electronic 'hacker' Net News group alt.2600 concerned the subject of hacking into the computerised legal retrieval service *Lexis*. For those hoping to reduce *Lexis* costs, the advice given was disappointing. The best strategy suggested was to stroll into a local university and 'shoulder surf' a password from an unsuspecting user. This tried and tested method remains a favourite for those pursuing the intentionally darker side of 'hacking'. Many other 'hacks' are still almost as quick and easy. During the Winter Olympics of 1994, the Net News carried many reports on how journalists had 'hacked' into Tonya Harding's e-mail account simply by using her date of birth. The links between credit card fraud and what is called 'hacking' are well-known, yet again the simplest methods are often the best. Before mail order companies tightened up security on mailing addresses, many such frauds were committed not by a generation of brilliant computer programmers overcoming the system security of credit card company databases, but by opportunists reading certain bulletin boards which posted account details of cards which had been stolen by more conventional means, thus making such information available to anyone with a computer and a modem. Obviously, any institution which relies on the digital transfer of credit, and which stores customer information on networked databases is at risk from the activities of 'hackers' but it is impossible to estimate to what extent skilled computer hackers are exploiting esoteric loopholes of operating systems in order to gain access to account information and to what extent the highways of Cyberspace are simply being used by criminals as a convenient means of communication. Some computer-using criminals may only have a working knowledge of computing and networking, others may possess next to none. No one expects a car thief necessarily to know more about a car than how to drive it and possibly a few ingenious tricks on overcoming car security, again probably acquired from a 'friend' rather than worked out from first principles; but few would possess the skills necessary to design and build a car. Many 'hackers' seeking financial gain from Cyberspace may well fall into the 'users' category rather than the designers. However, the opportunities available to those whose skills are of a higher calibre remain extremely lucrative and as use of networks as vehicles for the transportation of an increasing variety of goods and services increases, the stakes can only get higher.

Hacking in the 90s ?

This ad appeared in an edition of *Phrack* in March 1993.

Does this suggest that the golden age of 'hacking' has passed already ? What can we expect to see take its place? From 'phone phreaking' to 'hacking', what next ?

It might be thought that the worst examples of insecure systems belong to the past, to an age when the mere use of a password was expected to provide adequate security and that advances in technology and in security awareness have increased the readiness of system managers to respond to 'hacker' challenges. However, reports of threats to financial and military security are as frequent as ever with even sites which one might have expected to have adopted the best in security measures continuing to experience difficulties.

> For seven months the Pentagon has been unable to locate hackers tapping into its unclassified computer system, officials said Thursday. Defense Department officials have known since December that intruders in the United States and abroad have gained access to Pentagon computer files through the *Internet* and, in some cases, stolen, altered and erased records. But despite a security budget in the "hundreds of millions of dollars," the Pentagon has been unable to close the breach (*The Sun Herald*, 22 July 1994).

Is such activity evidence that *Phrack* style 'hacking' is still alive and well or is a 90s style of 'hacking' beginning to emerge? Are young 'hackers', who perhaps follow the distorted image of the 'media hacker', reaping where others have sown? Are latter day 'hackers' perhaps tempted by the fruits of 'hacking' rather than by the intellectual challenge? Computer networks now offer an increasing number of goods and services and as computer users turn into consumers, it is probable that rather than breaking into operating systems to explore the intricacies of system privileges, the 'hackers' of the future will be motivated by the desire to acquire the traffic on the 'Information Super Highway'. As computers themselves become high level consumer goods rather than low level technical 'gizmos', there will be more incentive to abuse the 'network' that operates in what is sometimes referred to as 'Cyberspace' rather than to target individual computers.

Packet Sniffing, Magic Cookies and Boxing

The lexicography of hacking has expanded since the days of Trojan Horses, Logic Bombs and Trapdoors. The names may have changed along with the technology but have the aims and motivations of 'hackers' changed to any great extent? To answer this question, we must look at the emergence of an electronic community known as the '*Internet*'.

The *Internet* is a complex web of interconnected sites whose communications is made possible by adherence to a shared protocol. Use of the *Internet* has multiplied exponentially with a current membership of approximately 20 million people, 2.5 million computers and 30,000 networks. In the good old days, use of the *Internet* was limited to academic and research institutions whose concerns on system security were minimal; after all the primary purpose of such a network was the open exchange of information. Data was sent from site to site, often via numerous intermediary sites, in small chunks known as packets. The packets were then re-assembled at the destination site in order to rebuild the complete message. As the focus shifts from individual sites to the network itself, such packets are extremely interesting and valuable to those seeking more than their fair share of network time and resources.

> The number of *Internet* sites compromised by the ongoing series of network monitoring (sniffing) attacks continues to increase. The number of accounts compromised world-wide is now estimated to exceed 100,000. This series of attacks represents the most serious *Internet* threat in its history (Computer Systems Consulting (CSC). WWW page spy.org).

Internet break-ins have been a national news story lately, with reports that in 1994 unknown intruders have purloined more than 10,000 passwords in a burst of activity during recent months. The Federal Bureau of Investigation is investigating, since so many "federal-interest computers" are attached to the wide-open *Internet* and since it is a crime to possess and use other peoples' passwords (*Newsday*, March 4th 1994).

Packet Sniffing is the latest piece of jargon to emerge in Cyberspace. 'Hackers' are now attacking networks themselves rather than targeting specific sites. 'Packet Sniffer' programs are installed which monitor traffic at public access *Internet* sites. User names and passwords can be winnowed out of the electronic chaff to yield valuable access rights. Such techniques can subvert all conventional attempts to secure passwords as even encrypted passwords may simply be 'replayed' to the intended host site, only 'use once and dispose' passwords within firewalls[3] can remain safe from the packet sniffers. Such activities may be carried out by system administrators attempting to assess site security, again blurring the distinction between 'hacking' or 'cracking' and legitimate system management. 'Magic Cookies', another addition to the hackers lexicography, are locations or addresses on the *Internet*. Many 'Magic Cookies' are public domain in any case, as on a gopher server[4] whose purpose is to provide a browsing facility for public domain information at that site. However some gopher servers may be open to abuse in that their actual domain may extend far beyond the menu, allowing illicit 'Magic Cookies' to be passed to it requesting information not intended for public access (Wallich 1994; also much discussed in the *Internet* newsgroup, alt.hackers).

The telecommunications network is still a target of contemporary hackers and indeed is estimated to be one of the fastest growing forms of network abuse although as always precise figures are difficult to gauge with estimates ranging from millions to billions of pounds each year. The incentives are lucrative: long distance calls are sold on to third parties, generating substantial revenues for the latter day phone phreakers. Methods vary from simple 'finger hacking', that is dialling at random until gold or an access code is struck, to manipulation of programmable chips on cellular phones. The 'phreaking' community is now no longer confined to the use of 'blue boxes'; devices which generated the necessary 2600 hertz. Phone system hackers can now choose from a variety of colour box devices - Aqua, Beige, Black, Blotto, Brown, Bud, Busy, Chartreuse, Cheese, Clear, Crimson, Gold, Jack, Neon, Paisley, Pandora's, Pearl, Red, Scarlet, Silver, Tron and Yellow. All these boxes carry out a specific hacking task: for example a pearl box is defined as

> a box that may substitute for many boxes which produce tones in hertz. The Pearl Box when operated correctly can produce tones from 1-9999hz. As you can see, 2600, 1633, 1336 and other crucial tones are obviously in its sound spectrum'(World WideWeb page).[5]

System Administrators or Hackers?

The introduction of World Wide Web[6] browsing software to the *Internet*[7] heightened the profile of 'hacker' oriented information. No longer hidden away on secret bulletin boards requiring aspiring 'hackers' to hunt for their numbers, pages such the following excerpt can be readily located

CLM Security Page
Security stuff:
- A beginners guide to cracking UNIX
- 8lgm mail hack for SunOS
- 81 gm passwd hack for SunOS

FTP Sites and file links:
- Security FTP site Connection — ftp.win.tue.nl
- Security FTP site (index of above site)
- cert.org ftp site.
- JHU site with papers such as Foiling_The_Cracker
- Crack program for cracking Unix passwords (ver 4.1).
- CrackerJack 1.4, Unix passwd cracker for DOS and OS/2

Christopher Menegay's Security Page, available on World Wide Web

New groups such as alt.2600, alt.hackers, alt.security, comp.security.unix (a small selection of system security/hacker oriented groups) regularly trade the latest discoveries and there are also numerous FTP[8] sites which carry backlogs of such information.

The *Internet* Underground, the latest addition to the World Wide Web collection of hacking information, begins with the following words

> Disclaimer: This page is provided for informational sake only. Don't do anything illegal. I don't.

Others may wonder why such information is posted to the *Internet* at all. Who is using such information and why ? Are they all conscientious system administrators honing their anti-hacking techniques or are they aspiring hackers looking for a nursery school environment to begin learning the tricks of the trade ? The answer may lie in exploring what is sometimes referred to as the 'hacker ethic'.

The Hacker Ethic

1. The belief that information sharing is a powerful positive good and that it is an ethical duty of hackers to share their expertise by writing free software and facilitating access to information and to computing resources wherever possible
2. The belief that system cracking for fun and exploitation is ethically acceptable as long as the cracker commits no theft, vandalism or breach of confidentiality.

(*As defined in The New Hacker's Dictionary.*)

The UK-based group, 8LGM (8 Legged Grove Machine), probably come within the second definition, although they themselves would argue that publicising system flaws is their only motivation. 8LGM is a self-appointed *Internet* security team which posts information to *Internet* news groups on security holes along with advice on how to exploit them. Their argument is that this is the best way to alert system managers and that overall, improved security will result. Others argue that 8LGM deliberately posts its articles at weekends, and that many systems are compromised before system managers arrive for work on Monday mornings. In addition to this many smaller sites continue to run old versions of the operating systems and continue to suffer even when 'known weaknesses' are fixed. The speed and the frequency with which such 'weaknesses' are publicised requires system managers to spend a great deal of time keeping in touch with the latest 'hacks'. This may explain the noticeable crossover between discussion of hacking and discussion of system security.

Example of an 8LGM post

```
Make copies of /etc/ passwd and /etc/ group, and modify them.
>     % id
      uid=97(8lgm) gid=97(8lgm) groups=97(8lgm)
>     % cp /etc/passwd /tmp/passwd
>     % ex /tmp/passwd
      /tmp/passwd: unmodified: line 42
>     :a
>     8lgmroot::0:0:Test account for lpr bug:/:/bin/csh
>     :wq
      /tmp/passwd: 43 lines, 2188 characters.
>     % cp /etc/group /tmp
>     % ex /tmp/group
      /tmp/group: unmodified: line 49
>     :/wheel
      wheel:*:0:root,operator
>     :c
      wheel:*:0:root,operator,8lgm
>     :wq
      /tmp/group: 49 lines, 944 characters.
Install our new files:
>     % ./lprcp /tmp/group /etc/group
>         ............................................ ........
      lpr: cannot rename /var/spool/lpd/cfA060testnode
>     % ./lprcp /tmp/passwd /etc/passwd
>         ............................................ ........
      lpr: cannot rename /var/spool/lpd/cfA061testnode
Check it worked:
>     % ls -l /etc/passwd /etc/group
```

```
      -rw-r—r— 1 8lgm    944 Mar 3 19:56 /etc/group
      -rw-r—r— 1 8lgm    2188 Mar 3 19:59 /etc/passwd
>     % head -1 /etc/group
      wheel:*:0:root,operator,8lgm
>     % grep '^8lgmroot' /etc/passwd
      8lgmroot::0:0:Test account for lpr bug:/:/bin/csh
Become root and tidy up:
>     % su 8lgmroot
      # chown root /etc/passwd /etc/group
      # rm -f /tmp/passwd /tmp/group
      #
```

NB This is only a very small excerpt from the necessary code and is an old hack which will not work on 'fixed' UNIX Operating Systems!

This is an example of a typical 'hack' - lines of code which if run on a certain version of UNIX will result in the 'hacker' gaining root privileges i.e. total control of the system. Hacking of this kind is analogous to chess playing: it requires the ability to think several steps ahead and to view the system or game mentally not as a linear one-dimensional structure but as a multi-dimensional system with infinite interrelationships. The system administrator's game is to run a secure system; however with oceans of code, all of which may be open to interesting new uses, it is a challenging task both to keep shipping lanes open for legitimate traffic and to keep out marauders. The strategy of the operating system hacker is to tweak out unforeseen dependencies and to exploit them.

8LGM, although no longer a 'hacker' group in the destructive sense of the word, has a chequered past. Two current members are Karl Strickland and Neil Woods who along with the more famous, 'addicted to hacking' Paul Bedworth were charged under the Computer Misuse Act in 1991. Many reformed hackers do go on to work as system managers, so it is not a particularly surprising career development, but could their activities still be a potential source of danger even if they themselves do not intend any destructive hacking?

Hackers may well not intend to cause harm to the computing system. Most indeed, have great respect for the code of the operating system but by not only discovering security loopholes but publishing them indiscriminately, they may be aiding the less well intentioned. Such hackers are perhaps motivated by belief in their superior programming ability and a belief that they alone hold the key to system security; that the computer world needs them. The reality may be very different: despite reports suggesting that Robert Morris was a brilliant if misguided programmer, it appears from later analyses[9] that the worm code he produced was sloppy and despite involving some clever tricks was hardly evidence of either original and ingenious code or superior programming intellect.

What motivates such 'hackers'? Why do they seek to discover holes in security systems when not specifically employed to do so and why do they make the information freely available to the world community via the *Internet* rather than simply alert system managers? It could also be argued that many system managers, particularly those running small systems, cannot afford to spend time and money implementing an endless series of patches and fixes. House owners would not welcome burglars whose activities required them to change their locks every two or three weeks because their flaws had been widely publicised.

Why do so many hackers believe that their activities are of benefit to system managers? Are their investigations into operating system security motivated by the desire to help or are they publicity seekers anxious to advertise their skills? Even if the latter is the case, does this necessarily imply that such people are dangerous? This may depend on how effective the 'hacking' advice is and to whom it is distributed. A person with legitimate concerns on airport security might, for a publicity stunt, smuggle an unattended package into a departure hall or attempt to check through unaccompanied packages. Sympathy for such a safety campaigner might be reduced if he or she decided to publicise the security loophole on a *Internet* News group before alerting the airport managers.

Hacking, Cracking or Committing Crime

'Hackers' can probably be divided into three main categories:

1. Hackers: Programmers, may investigate 'loopholes'. No malicious intent.
2. Crackers: Unwanted nuisances, may not be themselves malicious but may publicise their findings, enabling the malicious to attack system.
3. Those who commit further offences such as credit card fraud and misuse of the telecommunications system.

Some 'hackers' may fit easily into one particular category; others operate in a twilight zone between the categories . Those in the third category are the most obvious threat to an emerging 'Information super highway' which aims to provide an electronic on line 'Aladdin's Cave' to the modern consumer. Much more than 'free' long distance phone calls may become available to the contemporary robbers. Hackers may no longer have to circumvent mail order security when they use stolen credit card accounts; goods and services in electronic form may be diverted in transit; and perhaps a variant of a magic cookie could be used to persuade e-mail order catalogues to yield up their wares. Network abuse may provide opportunities for those who would not have considered conventional theft to commit a more anonymous and invisible form of crime. Most people in the first two categories would not go on to use their knowledge in this way but their eager desire to communicate their findings to a wider world community may well provide starting blocks for the less well intentioned. It may well be argued that genuine concerns on system security do not need to publicised on the *Internet* and that system operators could be warned more discreetly. Followers of this practice would argue that their motives are not self publicity but a desire to 'warn' the public quickly of the new danger and that there is no other practical way to contact thousands of system operators. This kind of hacker or cracker might well say that they are not creating the problem, that hacking is going on with or without on line tutorials, but that they are merely aiding system managers in their fight to keep the third category of hackers out.

Many such 'hackers' may be at worst attention-seeking self-important nuisances but by publicising their findings in such an free environment as the *Internet*, the danger is that others will follow, not merely to learn programming tricks in order to enhance their knowledge but to put their knowledge to more practical uses. As the *Internet* becomes more commercial, its wares may attract more buyers but it may well attract more electronic shoplifters.

Crime in Cyberspace

The term cyberspace was first used by the science fiction author William Gibson in his novel *Nuromancer* (1982) to describe the environment within which computer hackers operate. In the novel, the activity of hacking - securing unauthorised access to the contents of computer systems - is couched in very physical terms. The image is of the hacker overcoming physical security barriers to penetrate into the heart of computer systems and make changes to the physical structure, thereby modifying the operation of the system. When departing, the hacker might even remove and take away elements of the system.

Usage of physical terminology to describe aspects of computer technology is becoming commonplace. Much has been written concerning the concept of virtual reality. This immerses the user in a computer-generated world where every "action" taken by the user produces an appropriate feedback affecting all the senses. Virtual reality techniques are currently used by architects to enable users to inspect a building before a brick has been laid. Scientists use virtual reality techniques to "see" how molecular structures are composed and the effect of any changes. For the future, virtual reality techniques are set to move into the entertainment field; more lurid reports expound upon the possibilities of virtual reality sex. The promise - or threat - is that we can spend portions of our lives in 'virtual' worlds which will be indistinguishable from the real one save in the removal of any element of physical danger and in the ability of the user to exert a greater degree of control over the outcome of any exploits.

Whilst the use of physical descriptions may represent accurately the sentiments of those involved in the creation and use of computer-based technologies, it is much more doubtful how far the criminal law can or should regard simulation as indistinguishable from reality. Although a computer hacker's reach may extend across the world, the hacker never leaves the confines of his or her own keyboard. No matter how exotic an experience in virtual reality might be, the subject never leaves a particular physical location.

Although the computer world may exist only in intangible form, it affects and in some cases controls our physical environment and lives to a very significant extent. The airplane which takes us on holiday will have many of its functions controlled by computer. Conduct which adversely affects the operation of the computer will put the safety of the passengers in very real danger. The financial world is heavily dependent on computers. In our inter-dependent society it has been estimated that a prolonged failure of the computer system of a major bank in California would affect the economy of the state within 3 days, the United States within a week and the world within 28 days. Fortunately, the matter has not been put to the test.

The term 'computer virus' has entered into popular demonology. The essence of a computer virus is that, like its human equivalent, it may be transmitted from one computer to another. This may occur when an infected disk is transferred between computers. In the event that computers are linked together either in a network or using a telecommunications connection, the virus may also be transmitted electronically. Having infected a computer, the effects of viruses may vary widely. Some viruses are relatively benign. An example is the 'ping-pong' virus whose effects are limited to causing the image of a bouncing ball to move continually across the computer screen. Others such as the 'Friday 13th' and 'Michaelangelo' viruses[10] can result in the permanent loss of data stored on the victim computer. In one of the most notorious instances reported from the United States, a student at Cornell University wrote a computer program referred to as a worm. A worm is a program which replicates itself. Although initially it may produce few adverse effects, the continuing doubling in size begins to consume larger and larger amounts of the computer system's memory. Ultimately, it will consume the storage space available and, by overwriting material which is already there, will cause the loss of that data. In the case in question, the worm was let loose on the *Internet*. Within a matter of hours, 6,000 computers were affected across the United States. Almost as worryingly, the student, who ultimately was convicted under the United States Computer Fraud and Abuse Act 1986, did not set out with the intention of causing damage. The incident can best be described as a practical joke which went wrong. A deliberate attempt to maximise the damage could have produced far more serious effects.

One aspect of reports of the incident reveals a problem which besets efforts to assess the severity of computer related crime. One commentator assessed the cost of the "damage" at $186 million. Another, no less plausible estimate reduces the cost to a few thousand dollars. It would appear that in some instances, the involvement of the computer in any scheme prompts the addi-tion of several zeros to any assessment of the damage caused. In another case in the United States, a number of computer hackers were charged with theft of data from a telephone company. It was alleged that the value of the data was a very precise $79,499. This was based upon a calculation of all the costs incurred in compiling the data in question. The defence, however, was able to produce in evidence a technical document sold by the telephone company. This contained an even more extensive version of the data allegedly taken from the computer and retailed for $13. In the particular case, the prosecution collapsed at this point but the incident does indicate some of the difficulty which will be encountered whenever the attempt is made to put a value upon intangibles. The problem may not be as significant in Scotland where the offence itself is not dependent upon the value of the property involved.

The incidents recounted above serve as the basis for the first elements of this section. Initial consideration will be given to the extent to which those responsible for the destruction or amendment of data, whether by means of a computer virus or through other techniques, may face criminal sanctions. Next, consideration will be given to the legal response to the actions of computer hackers. In many instances, of course, the two topics will be linked and one of the features of the Law Commission's report[11] prior to the enactment of the Computer Misuse Act was its assertion that fear as to the possible harm resulting from an incident of computer hacking justified the imposition of criminal sanctions even though no actual harm had resulted.

Damage to Data

One of the first reported cases concerning damage to computer data was the English authority of *Cox v Riley* 83 Cr App R 54 (1986). The appellant had been employed to operate a powered saw. Although the device could be used in the traditional manner, it was also equipped with an early form of computer control. Printed circuit cards containing programs could be inserted into a processing unit and would allow the saw to operate automatically, cutting in accordance with pre-determined patterns. There was also a facility referred to as a "program cancellation function". When a particular button was depressed, the programs would be deleted from any card currently in use. The intention was that this facility would be used when the need for a particular pattern had terminated. Deleting the program would allow the card to be re-programmed with a new set of instructions in much the same way as one piece of music may be deleted from a cassette tape and replaced by another recording. Acting without authority and for no valid reason, the appellant deliberately operated the program cancellation function and erased a number of programs.

A more recent authority, *Denco v Joinson* [1992] 1 All ER 463, illustrates that misuse of computing facilities will generally constitute gross industrial misconduct justifying summary dismissal of the employee responsible. In many cases this may be considered the most appropriate response to instances of this kind, a view supported by surveys of computer misuse conducted by the Audit Commission for England and Wales. Even in cases of fraud involving computer systems, prosecutions resulted in only 42%[12] of cases. In *Cox v Riley*, however, criminal charges were brought alleging breach of section one of the Criminal Damage Act 1971. This states: A person who without lawful excuse destroys or damages any property belonging to another intending to destroy or damage any such property .. shall be guilty of an offence (section 1).

The word "property" is defined as "property of a tangible nature whether real or personal" (section 10).

The appellant, having been convicted before the magistrates, appealed on the point whether damage to property had occurred. No damage had been caused to any piece of physical property. Although the contents of the printed circuit card had been erased, it remained a viable storage device. Upholding the conviction, the Divisional Court held that the requirement of damage to property had been satisfied in that the owner of the saw, which was unquestionably property for the purpose of the statute, had been required to expend time and effort of a more than minimal amount in order to restore it to its original condition, i.e. a saw capable of cutting in accordance with the instructions contained in a computer program.

Basing the offence upon the effort required to return property to its original condition does not appear conceptually inconsistent with other forms of conduct held criminal. In the event that a person sprays paint on a wall, there is no doubt that the offence will have been committed. The wall, however, will not have been destroyed or weakened in any way and remains fit for its purpose. The only cost incurred will be that which has to be met by the owner in returning it to its original condition as a structure free from unwanted artistic works.

In the Scottish case of *HMA v Wilson* 1984 SLT 117 a similar approach was adopted in respect of the equivalent offence of malicious mischief. The case concerned a nuclear power station rather than a computer, it being alleged that the respondent had maliciously pushed an emergency stop button thereby causing cessation of electricity generation and a loss to his employers estimated at £147,000. The emergency stop button reset itself automatically and the effect of its operation was to stop the generating machinery in a normal and non-damaging fashion. The only loss suffered was economic in nature. Reversing the finding of the sheriff that the charge was irrelevant, the High Court ruled (Lord Stewart dissenting) that conduct depriving the owner of property of the opportunity to use it "productively and profitably" sufficed to found a charge of malicious mischief.

The application of the offence of criminal damage to computer related conduct was again at issue in the case of *R v Whitely* (1991) 93 Cr App Rep 25. This case is of considerable interest in that it was concerned with what might be regarded as classic attributes of computer hacking. Reference has previously been made to computer networks. The computing facilities at most United Kingdom institutes of higher education are linked in a network referred to under the acronym JANET (Joint Academic Network). The communications facilities associated with this network allowed a user connected at one site to obtain access to any other JANET site. Access to the network was controlled by passwords. Although Whiteley had no entitlement to access the system, the culture within academic computing facilities in the 1980s was such that security was not afforded high priority. The initial act of obtaining access to a computer system would not have been very difficult and the appellant was able to secure this using a very cheap and basic personal computer and modem set up in his home.

It is clear from the account given above that Whiteley's conduct had caused considerable inconvenience and not a little expense to the operators of the computer facilities affected and to other, authorised, users of the systems. Two charges were brought under the provisions of the Criminal Damage Act, the first alleging damage to the computer by virtue of their operations being stopped for periods of time, the second alleging damage to the discs (*sic*) which held the programs and data used in the computers. These discs are constructed to contain millions of magnetic particles which provide a medium for the recording of information in much the same way as a piece of paper can be written on. The effect of "writing" data to a disk is to produce particular combinations of magnetic polarity. These correspond to the binary symbols which form the basis of all digital computer operations. Whiteley's activities, it was argued, altered the make-up of magnetic particles causing impairment to the operation of the computer systems and thereby committing the offence of criminal damage.

The charge of criminal damage to the computers was dismissed by the jury, a verdict of which the Court of Appeal indicated its approval. A conviction on the second count for which Whiteley was sentenced to a term of 12 months imprisonment was the subject of the appeal, it being argued that the Criminal Damage Act required that damage be tangible. This contention was rejected by the Court of Appeal, the Lord Chief Justice (Lane) stating:

> It seems to us that that contention contains a basic fallacy. What the Act requires to be proved is that tangible property has been damaged, not necessarily that the damage itself should be tangible. There can be no doubt that the magnetic particles upon the metal discs were a part of the discs and if the appellant was proved to have intentionally and without lawful excuse altered the particles in such a way as to cause an impairment of the value or usefulness of the disc to the owner, there would be damage within the meaning of section 1. The fact that the alteration could only be perceived by operating the computer did not make the alterations any the less real, or the damage, if the alteration amounted to damage, any less within the ambit of the Act....If the hacker's actions do not go beyond, for example, mere tinkering with an otherwise "empty" disc, no damage would be established. Where, on the other hand, the interference with the disc amounts to an impairment of the value or usefulness of the disc to the owner, then the necessary damage is established.

The decision in *Whitely* represents authoritative endorsement of the view that an act causing amendment to data held on a computer storage device can constitute the offence of criminal damage. However, by the time the decision was handed down, the Computer Misuse Act 1990 had come into force. Acting on the expressed opinion of the Law Commission (1989) that:

> ... the practical meaning of damage has caused practical as well as theoretical problems ... evidenced by the experience of the police and prosecuting authorities who have informed us that, although convictions have been obtained in serious

cases of unauthorised access to data or programs, there is recurrent (and understandable) difficulty in explaining to judges, magistrates and juries how the facts fit in with the present law of criminal damage....

the Computer Misuse Act amended the Criminal Damage Act, providing in section 3(6) that:

> For the purposes of the Criminal Damage Act 1971 a modification of the contents of a computer shall not be regarded as damaging any computer or computer storage medium unless its effect on the computer or computer storage medium impairs its physical condition.

The provisions of the Computer Misuse Act will be discussed in more detail below. Two comments may be made at this stage concerning the approach adopted. First, nowhere does the 1990 Act make any amendment to Scots criminal law. There would appear no reason why a charge of malicious mischief or vandalism could not continue to be brought in respect of computer-related conduct. A second point to note is that the amendment to the Criminal Damage Act applies in respect of "the contents of a computer". Although this definition includes any disks or other forms of storage medium which are permanently or temporarily incorporated in a computer, the Act does not apply to a storage device *per se*. In the event that an unauthorised person placed a magnet in close proximity to a disk thereby causing the loss of any data held on it, no offence would be committed under the Computer Misuse Act, as the disk could not be regarded as forming a part of a computer at the relevant time. Any prosecution would have to have recourse to the much-maligned Criminal Damage Act (as indeed would any prosecution based on the allegation that the contents of an audio or video tape had been erased). Such a dichotomy appears likely to perpetuate the educative problems referred to by the Law Commission. It cannot be considered satisfactory that conduct which produced exactly the same effect should face different criminal sanctions depending upon the accident whether a disk is in or out of a computer at the relevant time. Especially given the clear pronouncements of the Court of Appeal in *Whitely*, it might have been preferable to restrict any amendment to the definition of property in the Criminal Damage Act, making it clear that damage to the contents of any storage device would constitute damage to the device itself.

Unauthorised Access to Data

The essence of the cases and the issues described in the preceding section is that conduct deprives the owner of an object of the opportunity to use it in the manner desired. The next form of conduct to be considered is that whereby an unauthorised person seeks only to obtain access to, and normally a copy of, information held in a computer system. Two situations will be considered in this context. The first occurs when the owner of a data base is willing to make access available upon payment of specified fees, only for a party to attempt to access the system whilst evading payment. In the second situation, the data user does not wish to make the information available to the world at large and, again, is the subject of the attentions of a computer hacker.

Undoubtedly the best known case involving the legal response to computer hacking is that of *R v Gold* [1988] AC 1063. Gold, together with his co-accused Schifreen, was a computer hacker. The victim in the case at issue was British Telecom who operated a computer service *Prestel*. The system consisted of a central computer system which provided a considerable variety of computer-related services to its subscribers including electronic mail. Subscribers would be issued with a password and a user identification code. This would allow the system to monitor the extent of their usage and charge them accordingly. Special passwords were issued to British Telecom employees who required to access the system for the purposes of their employment. The attraction of these passwords for a would-be hacker was that they did not cause any bills to be generated. Gold discovered such a password and made extensive use of it before the fact of his conduct was discovered.

If the case had originated in Scotland, there is little doubt that a charge of obtaining services by means of a false pretence would have been competent. Such a charge looks at the actions and intentions of the party seeking the service. In this case there seems no doubt that the hackers were seeking to masquerade as authorised users for the purpose of obtaining free access to the services. In England, the Theft Act 1968 had replaced the concept of false pretence with that of obtaining services by deception. This change followed the recommendations of the Criminal Law Revision Committee whose eighth report sought to place greater emphasis upon the effect which conduct had upon its victim. The difficulty with this approach in the computer context is the question whether a machine can be deceived. Although there are no clear *dicta* on the point, the prevailing opinion appeared to be that the answer lay in the negative. Faced with uncertainty on this critical point, the decision was made to bring charges under the Forgery and Counterfeiting Act of 1981. This Act contained a number of provisions which appeared to make it appropriate for the facts of the case. It provides that an offence is committed by a party who presents a false instrument with the intention that it should be taken as genuine. It is further provided that attempts to deceive a machine should be equated with those affecting a human.

Gold and Schifreen were convicted at trial, only for these convictions to be overturned by the unanimous judgments of the Court of Appeal and the House of Lords. The major objection identified by the appellate courts to the application of the Act lay in the difficulty of identifying any instrument which was used. The term "instrument" was defined in the Act as including any "disc, tape, sound track or other device in or one which information was recorded or stored". This, it was held, restricted its application to the situation where there was some physical storage device. In the present case this could only occur where the password details transmitted by the appellants were recorded on the Prestel system. Two objections were taken to such a result. First, largely because of the special nature of the passwords used, no details were maintained beyond the brief period, less than one second, taken for the authenticity of the password to be verified by the system. This, it was held, was too short a period to constitute a recording as required in the Act. The second objection was to the necessary identification of the Prestel computer as both the source of the deception and its victim. A somewhat schizophrenic state of affairs. Most damningly perhaps, both tribunals were critical of the attempt to invoke the Forgery and Counterfeiting Act, the Lord Chief Justice commenting:

> We have accordingly come to the conclusion that the language of the Act was not intended to apply to the situation which was shown to exist in this case. It is a conclusion which we reach without regret. The Procrustean attempt to force these facts into the language of an Act not designed to fit them produced great difficulties for both judge and jury which we would not wish to see repeated ... The appellants' conduct amounted in essence .. to dishonestly obtaining access to the relevant Prestel data bank by a trick. That is not a criminal offence. If it is thought desirable to do so, that is a matter for the legislature rather than the courts. We express no view on the matter.

The failure of the prosecution in this case was widely regarded as leaving the owners of the burgeoning ranks of commercial data bases exposed to the predatory activities of hackers and served to fuel the existing calls for legislative reform. It is likely that similar conduct might now be prosecuted under the provisions of section one of the Computer Misuse Act 1990.

Theft of Information

In situations such as that at issue in *R v Gold* the computer owner's loss may be expressed in terms of the access charges normally levied. In the situation where a user does not wish third parties to obtain access to data, the effect of such conduct may be more serious from the "victim's" perspective than that where data is altered or erased. An efficient user will ensure that "back up" copies are maintained of all programs and data (subject to possible copyright problems as described in Chapter 4). Destruction of one copy of the data may then cause only temporary inconvenience. As was stated in the recent Canadian case of *R v Stewart* 149 DLR (3d) 583 (1983):

> Compilations of information are often of such importance to the business community that they are securely kept to ensure their confidentiality. The collated confidential information may be found in many forms covering a wide variety of topics ... For many businessmen their confidential lists may well be the most valuable asset of their company.

A domestic illustration of this phenomenon can be seen in the case of *Grant v. Allan* 1987 SCCR 402 where the respondent removed a quantity of computer printouts from his employer's premises. The business in question was a parcel and document delivery service and the information on the printouts related to its customers and its pricing policy. The value of such information to a competitor is self-evident. The fact of the accused's conduct came to light when he approached one competitor with the offer to sell the information for £400, this approach subsequently being reported to the police and the accused arrested when he attempted to complete the transaction.

The major difficulty facing any prosecution in such a situation is the perennial issue whether information might be regarded as property sufficient to found a charge of theft. In the English case of *Oxford v Moss* (1978) 68 Cr App R 183 a university student discovered a proof copy of an examination paper which he was due to attempt. He removed the paper with the intention of copying it. Realising that if the paper's absence were discovered a different paper might be set, it was an integral part of his scheme that the copy would be returned. The student was caught in the act of returning the paper. Under the Theft Act 1968, an essential element of the offence was the intention that the owner be deprived permanently of the property involved. This, of course, was not the case and so the student could not be charged with theft of the paper. In the event, a charge was brought alleging theft of the confidential information contained in the paper. It may well be argued, of course, that the "owner" was not deprived of the confidential information although the fact of the student's conduct might be taken as destroying the element of confidentiality. In the event, however, the charge was dismissed by the magistrates whose finding that confidential information could not be regarded as property under the Theft Act was upheld by the Divisional Court.

Although a different approach has been adopted in a number of cases emanating from the United States where information has been accepted as constituting the subject of theft, these have been derived from a definition of theft significantly different from that applied in England and Scotland[13]. In Canada, although the majority of the Court of Appeals held in the case of *R v Stewart* that confidential information could be regarded as property, this view was rejected by a unanimous Supreme Court. As *Oxford v Moss* illustrates, problems involving the property status of information did not await the computer. Espionage is generally regarded as one of the older professions. Although *Oxford v Moss* illustrates that this is not always the case, such conduct often involves the perpetrator in the commission of offences involving unauthorised access to property-burglary, obtaining entry to a lockfast place etc. In the situation where information is held on a computer and where access may be obtained by means of a telecommunications link, there is no need for a computer spy to set foot on the premises. In the situation where personal data is involved, salt may even be rubbed into the victim's wounds when it is discovered that a breach of the eighth data protection principle requiring the maintenance of adequate security has been committed and the wrath of the Data Protection Registrar must be faced. With only limited exaggeration, the consequence may be analogised to prosecuting a house owner whose property has been burgled for failing to secure windows or doors whilst exculpating the burglar.

In the situation where an unauthorised party has secured access to data held on a computer system with the view to obtaining some advantage from this conduct, there has been a widespread recognition that the conduct should attract criminal sanctions as a form of electronic burglary. Both the Council of Europe, which produced a report concerning the need for and basic form of computer crime legislation, and the Scottish Law Commission made recommendations to this effect, the latter recommending the enactment of a Computer Crime (Scotland) Act. This would have created one new offence committed by a person who:

> ... not having authority to access to a program or data stored in a computer ... obtains such unauthorised access in order to inspect or otherwise to acquire knowledge of the program or the data or to add to, erase or otherwise alter the program or the data with the intention:
>
> (a) of procuring an advantage for himself or another person; or
>
> (b) of damaging another person's interests.

Few would dispute the desirability of prosecuting the theft of data from a computer system on the same basis as existing property-related offences. More controversial is the question whether the unadorned act of obtaining access to data held on a computer should be criminalised. The challenge of hacking for many actors, it is suggested, lies in the act of obtaining access to computer systems. Effectively, the goal is to see how far the hacker can travel from his own keyboard. The nature of the information held on any systems visited is of little interest, the journey being the end in itself.

The Scottish and English Law Commissioners disagreed on the question whether unauthorised access should be criminalised. The Law Commission, which in its initial Working Paper had expressed doubt on the point, explained in the final Report that it had changed its opinion following confidential briefings from computer users. These indicated that even though a hacker may not have been acting with any ulterior motive, the conduct could cause serious loss to the user. In the event of discovery that an unauthorised party had obtained access to a computer system, it was argued, the user would very likely be unaware of the extent of the penetration and of any changes which may have been made to the contents of the system. Even inadvertently, an unauthorised user might cause the corruption or erasure of programs or data held on the system whilst the possibility that deliberate harm, involving perhaps the insertion of logic bombs or the introduction of a computer virus, could never be discounted. A user faced with evidence of unauthorised access would have to assume the worst. In an example cited to and by the Law Commission a user expended some 10,000 hours of staff time rebuilding a computer system on becoming aware that an unauthorised person had obtained access. Faced with such evidence, the Law Commission recommended that the act of obtaining unauthorised access should be criminalised.

Such an approach raises a number of issues of principle which serve to illustrate yet more of the difficulties which the law faces in attempting to regulate aspects of computer-related conduct. It has been argued on a number of occasions in this work that the law fails to take adequate account of the fact that intangible property is as valuable an asset as any more tangible commodity. If comparison is made with other forms of property and behaviour, it will be seen that the effect of the Law Commission's recommendation is to confer an exalted status upon data held in a computer system. Save under the provisions of the Official Secrets Acts, if confidential information is written on a piece of paper which is left on top of a desk visible through a window, no offence would be committed by a person who looked at the document through the window. No offence indeed would be committed by a person who took a photograph of the document and its contents. Although the situation may be less certain, it is possible that a similar conclusion would apply where a document is left in an unlocked office or house and a unauthorised person entered the premises to read or photograph it. There may, of course, be legal ramifications under the law of copyright, but no criminal offence will be committed. As a general rule, the mere act of obtaining access to property does not constitute an offence. This occurs only where security measures are overcome or where property is damaged or removed.

The argument that criminal sanctions should be imposed because a computer user is put to expense in consequence of a feeling of apprehension that damage may have occurred also appears to lack precedent. If a house owner becomes aware that house keys have disappeared for a period of time and then reappeared, she may well be concerned that an unauthorised party has copied the keys. A reasonable response to this fear might see locks being changed at not inconsiderable expense and inconvenience. Assuming that the person responsible for the keys' removal is discovered and that it transpires that no copy was made, it may be doubted whether any criminal offence has been committed. A more extreme example might be an airline becoming aware that an unauthorised party has accessed a plane's engines. If the response were to be other than grounding the plane pending exhaustive checks, it is likely that the airline would be considered negligent. Again, if it transpired that no damage had been caused, the expense and inconvenience caused would not of itself give rise to any criminal sanctions.

The Computer Misuse Act 1990

Unusually for a measure concerned solely with the imposition of criminal sanctions, the Computer Misuse Act 1990 was introduced as a Private Members Bill. At the time of the Law Commission's report, it was contemplated that legislative proposals might be announced in the Queen's Speech and to facilitate this, the Commission advanced publication of their report to such an extent that it did not follow the normal procedure of appending a draft Bill.

The Computer Misuse Act draws almost entirely upon the Law Commission's Report. Although the legislation applies to Scotland, the work of the Scottish Law Commission was disregarded under the explanation that the rapid pace of change in computer-related fields lent extra authority to the more recent deliberations of the English body. Given the radical differences between the two reports and the fact that they were separated by less than 2 years in time, this explanation cannot support an optimistic prognosis for the effectiveness of the 1990 Act.

The legislation creates three new offences. Section 1 renders criminal the attempt to obtain unauthorised access to programs or data held on a computer. Section 3 applies in the situation where the contents of a computer system are subjected to an unauthorised modification. Section 2 attempts to deal with another aspect of computer related behaviour, namely the speed with which conduct can move from preparation to perpetration. Under the normal law of criminal attempts, a person can only be charged with an attempted offence when he moves beyond the stage of preparing to commit an offence to that of attempting to put the plans into practice. The dividing line between preparation and perpetration has always proved difficult to draw but the Law Commission accepted the argument that the speed with which operations might be accomplished using a computer was such as to justify bringing forward the moment in time at which a serious criminal offence is committed. The calculation that the foreign currency reserves could be transferred electronically in 15 minutes has been cited already. Attempting to discover the combination of a bank safe is some way removed from the attempt to stage a robbery. Attempting to discover the codes and combinations used to effect an electronic fund transfer may leave the party involved with only a minor amount of work to do in order to complete the criminal scheme. The attempt to discover the codes might be considered as analogous to the attempt to use the knowledge of the combination to open the safe in the more old-fashioned example.

Although the above example provides reasonable justification for legislative intervention, a further hypothesis advanced by the Law Commission reveals a difficulty associated with *ad hoc* and computer-specific legislation. This example concerned the situation when a hacker attempted to gain access to the computerised medical records of patients suffering from the AIDS virus with the intention of using the information acquired for blackmail purposes. The Commission postulated that at the stage of attempting to obtain access the scheme would not have advanced sufficiently to found a charge of attempted blackmail. Accepting that this is the case, the question may be put how far the involvement of the computer serves to change anything. In the banking example cited above, it is clear that the computerised robber is enabled to advance the criminal scheme to a greater extent than his or her traditional counterpart. The computerised blackmailer secures no similar advantage. As has been said in the context of the Data Protection Act, the fact of the computer's involvement is purely fortuitous.

The Unauthorised Access Offence

The preceding discussion has concentrated upon the desirability of making unauthorised access illegal *per se*. Attention will now be given to the likely effectiveness of the approach adopted within the Computer Misuse Act.

Section 1 provides that a person shall be guilty of an offence if:

(a) he causes a computer to perform any function with intent to secure access to any program or data held in any computer;

(b) the access he intends to secure is unauthorised; and

(c) he knows at the time when he causes the computer to perform the function that this is the case.

Commission of the unauthorised access offence attracts a maximum penalty of a six-month term of imprisonment and a fine of £2,000. This amount is twice that recommended by the Law Commission.

A number of features of the offence call for comment. In common with the generally adopted approach, no attempt is made to define the word computer. Given the proliferation of micro-processors in every day appliances such as motor cars, washing machines and video recorders the ambit of the legislation is exceptionally broad.

The two key elements of the definition are the requirement that the attempt be made to cause a computer to perform a function with the intention that this should enable access to be secured to any program or data stored in it. These phrases are themselves the subject of extensive definitions. Effectively, any action which causes the computer to operate in any way will come within the scope of section 1. In particular, access will be obtained to a program held in a computer when the program operates. It is not necessary that the user should see the program in question or that its operation should be internal to the computer. An example might concern a washing machine controlled by micro-processors. Any person using the washing machine would cause their operation, thereby obtaining access to the programs involved. If the use of the machine was unauthorised, a section 1 offence might be committed. Such a conclusion has to be set alongside the general rule that unauthorised use of an object is not, *per se*, criminal.

An offence will only be committed if the party seeking access knows that his or her efforts are unauthorised. Paradoxically, this may be more readily established in the case of unauthorised use of a washing machine than of a computer. The question of whether access is unauthorised will be determined by reference to the state of mind of the computer owner or of the person entitled to control access. In the case of computerised library catalogues where terminals are located throughout the library, it is likely to be the case that access is authorised to the world at large - or at least that portion entitled to enter the library. In other cases, the user may wish to authorise much more limited access and it may well be that the intention would be that no other person should be authorised to use the equipment. It should be stressed that decisions are to be made by a person entitled to control access. If a person is allocated a password allowing access to the system and reveals details of this to a third party thereby enabling them to obtain access, that access will be unauthorised as the party disclosing the necessary information is not author-ised to control access. Instances have been reported of computer bulletin boards displaying details of telephone numbers and passwords enabling access to be obtained to specific systems. The fact that the details are genuine will not make any subsequent use authorised.

The intention of the user is only one element of the statutory equation. In order to secure a conviction it must be established that an accused knew that his or her access was unauthorised. In the situation where access is obtained to the physical components of a computer, e.g. the user sits in front of and uses a keyboard attached to the computer, the question whether knowledge that access is unauthorised will be closely linked that whether the presence on the premises involved was authorised. Matters may not be resolved so simply when access is obtained remotely. This is more in line with the stereotypical view of hackers. The evidentiary burden of establishing knowledge that access was unauthorised is a heavy one. The fact that a party should have suspected that his attentions were unwanted would not suffice. Given the lack of case law under the 1990 Act any comment in this area must be speculative; but the scenario will be considered in which a hacker has been given a telephone number corresponding with a computer system and connects to the system. At that stage it is most unlikely that an offence will be committed under section 1. The first point of contact with a computer system is normally via a 'log in' screen. This will normally identify the system. At this stage the hacker may suspect that he is not authorised to make use of the system but suspicion may fall short of knowledge. It may well be that the log in screen will also make reference to the provisions of the Computer Misuse Act and state specifically that unauthorised access constitutes a criminal offence. It may well be that the inclusion of such a warning will suffice to establish the guilt of a person who has no access right but who seeks to move from the log in screen to explore the contents of the system itself.

Few computer systems of any significance will rely only upon warning notices as means for keeping unauthorised users at bay. In the same way as a house-owner will use locks and possibly burglar alarms, so security precautions will be built into the system. Typically, these involve allocating passwords to authorised users and requiring these to be inserted prior to allowing access to proceed. Although it may be likely that sight of a demand for a password should signify to a user that her presence is unauthorised, in some cases the requirement for a password is a matter of form rather than substance. Some systems will allow a user to obtain access using a password such as "guest" or "anonymous". Other systems (or system managers) impose very lax control over the choice of passwords. In the case of *Denco v Joinson*, for example, a Welsh employee selected the password "Taff". In the seminal case of *R v Gold*, the access information discovered by the accused was in two stages. First came a password which in this case consisted of the number 2 repeated eight times. This required to be followed by a user identification code which used the number 1234.

The difficulty of establishing knowledge will be even greater when a user possess limited access rights but where the allegation is that these have been exceeded. Typically, this may occur in an employment relationship. In *Denco v Joinson* for example, the appellant had been granted limited access to the computer system in connection with his employment as a metal worker but allegedly sought to access information relating to the firm's customers, information which fell outwith the scope of his access rights. The appellant's conduct in this case was compounded by the fact that he had made use of a password allocated to another employer. The computer culture existing within the workplace may be a matter of some importance in this respect. It was reported in *Denco* that in the initial stages of computerisation, management encouraged employees to make use of the computer even though this was not required for the performance of their duties. In such a climate, it might be difficult to establish the requisite knowledge.

The decision to make unauthorised access an offence has been criticised as marking an unwarranted extension to the criminal law. In practice, the manner in which it has been implemented in the Computer Misuse Act may render the issue of little practical importance The most difficult issue occurs when a user displays clear and unequivocal notices warning that unauthorised users are not welcome but takes no further security measures to prevent access. In such a situation, an offence may well be committed under the Act but it is difficult to reconcile this situation with the doomsday scenarios postulated by the Law Commission in which users, fraught with concern at the possible damage caused by intruders, incur enormous expenditure in rebuilding the system. The fact that users have been lax in incorporating or applying security precautions should not be seen as grounds for refusing protection. The fact that a lock can be forced easily does not provide any defence for a party so acting. By extending the scope of the prohibition so widely, the Act may protect those who might be considered little deserving, but by imposing the requirement of establishing knowledge may deny protection to those whose genuine attempts at maintaining security are defeated by conduct which may fairly be stigmatised as negligent or reckless but which might not readily be characterised as intentional. The issue will always be one of fact, but it may be difficult to ascribe knowledge to a hacker who was given access details by a friend or even found them on a bulletin board.

The Ulterior Intent Offence

As stated above, the goal of this offence is to bring forward in time the moment at which a serious criminal offence is considered to have been committed. To effect this, it is provided that:

> A person is guilty of an offence under this section if he commits an offence under section 1 above (the unauthorised access offence) with intent-
>
> (a) to commit an offence to which this section applies; or
>
> (b) to facilitate the commission of such an offence (whether by himself or any other person).

The offences referred to in paragraph (a) are those for which a term of imprisonment of 5 or more years might be imposed upon a person with no previous criminal record.

Commission of the unauthorised access offence is a pre-requisite for commission of the ulterior intent offence. This may serve to limit the practical utility of the new provision. Over the last decade, the Audit Commission has conducted triennial surveys attempting to discover the extent of the losses resulting from computer fraud and other forms of computer misuse. In most of the cases reported to the Commission, the losses resulted from internal causes. Although not included in these surveys, the case of *R v Thompson* [1984] 3 All ER 565 might be regarded as indicative of the behaviour involved.

Thompson was employed as a computer programmer by a bank in Kuwait. His work gave him access to the computer systems which held details of customers' accounts. Thompson devised a fraudulent scheme which involved programming the computers to transfer sums from such accounts into other accounts which he had opened in his own name. In an effort to avoid detection the transfers were not to be effected until Thompson had left the bank's employ and was literally on a plane returning to England. Upon his return, Thompson attempted to realise his gains by causing the apparent contents of his accounts to be transferred to another account which he had opened with an English bank. It was at this point that his conduct was discovered and Thompson was charged with obtaining property by deception.

The major legal point in this case concerned the question whether the English courts had jurisdiction in the matter, Thompson arguing that any offence had been committed in Kuwait. Rejecting this claim, the Court of Appeal held that the offence was committed only when Thompson secured control of the funds involved. Merely causing a credit balance to appear on his bank accounts did not suffice.

The facts in *Thompson* indicate the justification for the ulterior intent offence. Although a conviction was obtained, the effect of the decision would be to leave a bank vulnerable - or at least denied the protection of significant elements of the criminal law - until a fraudulent scheme was within seconds of completion. The difficulty might be to determine whether Thompson, or any other employee in a similar position, had committed the unauthorised access offence. A distinction exists between unauthorised access and unauthorised use of access. Although much will once again depend upon the facts of a particular case, it may be difficult to establish that an authorised user has stepped sufficiently far outside any access rights to commit the unauthorised access offence.

In the situation where the unauthorised access offence is committed with the requisite ulterior intent, this latter offence will also be committed even though it should transpire that it would be impossible to commit the later offence. An example might concern a person attempting to obtain access to codes or passwords used by a bank to authenticate electronic fund transfers without realising that further security measures would mean that possession of these items of information would not suffice to cause a transfer to be made.

The world-wide nature of telecommunications facilities brings a significant international dimension into all aspects of computer-related conduct. In terms of the jurisdiction of the United Kingdom authorities, the basic provision is that jurisdiction may be claimed either when the party involved or the victim computer system is located within a domestic jurisdiction. This poses comparatively few definitional problems concerning the unauthorised access offence or with the unauthorised modification offence which will be considered in more detail below. Matters are not so straightforward where the conduct which allegedly constitutes the ulterior intent offence possesses an international dimension. The case of *Thompson* again provides an apposite illustration of such a situation. The approach adopted in the Computer Misuse Act is to confer jurisdiction upon the relevant domestic tribunals both where all aspects of the conduct occur within the jurisdiction and where it is intended to commit the further offence in some other jurisdiction, subject to the condition that the conduct would be regarded as possessing a sufficient element of criminality in the relevant legal system. In cases of fraud or theft it is likely that these requirements will be satisfied almost regardless of where the conduct is envisaged to occur. The position may be more complicated where the further offence relates to damage to data, perhaps by disseminating a computer virus. It will be recalled that the Law Commission expressed concern at the problems encountered in the application of the existing provisions of the Criminal Damage Act. Where other jurisdictions have not enacted any form of computer misuse statute, it may be that difficulties will be encountered in establishing that the conduct is regarded as criminal in the jurisdiction involved.

The Unauthorised Modification Offence

The third new offence created by the Computer Misuse Act is designed to substitute for the invocation of the Criminal Damage Act. The offence will be committed by a person who intentionally commits any act which alters the contents of a computer system in such a manner as to impair its operation. Once again, it is to be noted that the offence may be committed only by a party who acts intentionally. Negligent or even reckless conduct will not suffice.

In order to commit the offence it is not necessary that a party makes any form of contact with a computer. A person who creates a computer virus and puts it into circulation will, assuming the necessary intention can be established, commit the unauthorised modification offence in respect of each computer system affected.

Few would dispute the validity of the attempt to impose criminal sanctions upon those who seek deliberately to impair the operations of a computer system. As stated above, programs and data are protected under the Computer Misuse Act only whilst they are stored in a computer system. It is arguable that the provision is framed sufficiently broadly to encompass forms of activity which would not normally be considered as criminal. The example might be cited of a person who types a personal letter using a word processing system belonging to his or her employer. By adding data to the contents of the system, a modification is undoubtedly being performed. The user must be taken to have intended to make such a modification. It is immaterial for the purposes of the Act whether the modification is permanent or merely temporary. All that remains is the question whether the modification has impaired the operation of the computer system. The answer to this may depend upon the nature of the computer system and the fact whether the employee causes a copy of the letter to be retained on the system. In general, however, the more data is held on a computer, the slower will be its functioning - even though the diminution in performance may not be perceptible to an ordinary user. The Act does not require that impairment be significant and, in principle, there would appear no reason why a charge should not be brought in such an instance. Given that mere use of property is not generally regarded as constituting a criminal offence, the effect may again be to put a computer owner in a specially protected position.

Conclusions

As more and more reliance is placed upon the computer in legitimate activities, so it is likely that it will serve increasingly both as a target of and tool for those whose motives and aspirations might generally be regarded as criminal. The Computer Misuse Act marks the first attempt to introduce specific controls but this approach carries with it the danger that it may treat as the exception activities which are becoming the rule. Certainly, the involvement of the computer may add new dimensions to existing topics but the most urgent need is to concentrate upon the substance of the conduct rather than the accident whether a computer is involved. The Home Affairs Committee of the House of Commons has recently published the report of its investigation into the topic of computer pornography (House of Commons 1993-4). Although it may be that the interactive possibilities made available in computer programs represent a novel feature, conceptually the manner in which information is generated and recorded should have nothing to do with the determination whether it is pornographic or not. One point that is well made in the evidence submitted to the Committee by the Greater Manchester police is that the ease with which data - in this case graphical images - may be transmitted by means of the telephone system imposes substantial limitations upon national law enforcement agencies. After observing that the United Kingdom's obscenity laws are more stringent than those prevailing in most other countries it comments "It is highly unlikely that the international community will alter their obscenity laws. We will be faced with the situation that if it is available somewhere, it will be available everywhere".

Responsibility for criminal matters has traditionally been regarded as a national matter. Even the European Union's reach, for example, does not extend into the sphere of criminal law. Cyberspace, however, is no respecter of national boundaries. The examples cited above indicate that as in other areas of law, there is urgent need for international co-operation and co-ordination. The comments of the Home Affairs Committee indicate that this may be no simple task.

Chapter Two

The Individual in the Computer Society

One of the most powerful images in literature is that of a society where individual privacy is subsumed to the desire for societal conformity. In works such as Thomas More's Utopia, the sacrifice of individual privacy is justified in the interest of the collective good. In other instances, such as the works of Franz Kafka, privacy is sacrificed in the interests of an anonymous ruling class. With George Orwell's seminal work *1984*, the use of technology added a new element to the surveillance society and it is, of course, with the technological aspects of the subject that this work will be concerned.

In the ongoing debate as to the appropriate legal response to data processing activities, the topic of privacy has been afforded a place of honour with the issues involved frequently being discussed under the heading of "informational privacy". Concentration on the issue of privacy may be a cause for some regret, especially in the United Kingdom where the right to privacy receives, at best, limited legal recognition. This is well illustrated by the recent English case of *Kaye v Robertson* [1991] FSR 62. The plaintiff, a well-known actor, had been hospitalised following a car accident. A journalist and photographer employed by the *Sunday Sport* newspaper secured through trickery access to the plaintiff's hospital room. Photographs were taken of the plaintiff which it was planned to publish in the *Sunday Sport* accompanying what purported to be an exclusive interview with him. An action was raised on the plaintiff's behalf seeking to enjoin publication of the story. Although the action ultimately met with partial success on other grounds, Bingham LJ expressed concern at the absence of any remedy based on infringement of privacy. "If ever a person has a right to be let alone by strangers with no public interest to pursue, it must surely be when he lies in hospital recovering from brain surgery, and in no more than partial command of his faculties. Yet it alone, however gross, does not entitle him to relief in English law".

There would appear no clear basis upon which a Scottish court could reach a different conclusion (cf Hogg 1994) and as will be apparent from discussion of the terms of the Data Protection Act, there is the real danger that attempting to build a system of legal protection upon the uncertain foundations of privacy produces a fragile structure. Prior to considering the provisions of this statute, this chapter will consider aspects of the use of personal information in order to identify the threats to individual freedoms which the legislation is intended to counter.

"Every breath you take"

Every action we take says something about ourselves. The time we go to bed and the time we get up in the morning says something about our life-style. The same can be said about the food and drink we purchase, the shops we frequent, the books and newspapers we buy or borrow from a library, the journeys we make, the diseases we catch, the television programmes we watch, the telephone calls we make. In previous eras, anyone wishing to discover this information would have to indulge in extensive physical surveillance. The prospect of being placed under this degree of scrutiny would be abhorrent to most people but the labour-intensive nature of the activities would mean that the effort could be directed only against a small percentage of the population. The recent introduction of surveillance cameras in public areas and of speed detection equipment on the highways indicates how technology is expanding the scale of physical surveillance. A further development is the ability to identify electronically car number plates and, albeit less effectively, particular individuals.

Although few of us might expect to be specifically targeted for physical surveillance, our own actions give out information to anyone who chooses to listen - a form of passive surveillance. It is impossible to live in society without interacting with other people and purchasing goods and services. A person purchasing a train ticket to travel from Glasgow to Edinburgh necessarily engages in a degree of interaction with staff at the ticket office. It would be a nonsense for travellers to argue that their privacy had been violated because the ticket clerk became aware of their travel plans. In the same manner, we have to accept that a shop assistant will see what we buy, and that a librarian will issue books to us. Entering into perhaps more controversial territory, we recognise that the telephone company will have to be told the number which we wish to call and, in an age of itemised billing, will require to retain details for billing purposes.[1] At present, the television example is more remote, although the tendency with satellite broadcasting appears to be moving away from the situation where the viewer subscribes to a particular channel or channels to one where individual programmes are selected on a "pay as you view" basis. Such a system already operates in certain areas of the United States. In one extensively reported case, a cinema owner faced prosecution for showing an obscene film. It transpired that the film had also been broadcast by the local cable television service which operated a payment system as described above. As part of his defence, the cinema owner sought access to the viewing records of the broadcasting company with a view to citing viewers to testify that they had not been shocked or depraved as a result of viewing the film in question (Segal 1986).

We are used to the notion that we lead our lives in a series of compartments. In most of the examples cited above the range of dissemination is extremely limited. If I purchase a train ticket paying for the transaction with cash, the clerk will have some recollection of the transaction. The life span of the recollection may be limited and it is unlikely that he or she will be able to put a name against my face. If I pay by means of a cheque, then the potential range of dissemination increases and my name becomes identified with the transaction. If payment is made by credit or debit card using some form of EFTPOS (electronic fund transfer at the point of sale), the time and place at which the transaction took place will be recorded along with the identifying details and, perhaps, information as to the nature of the transaction itself.

This simple example illustrates how the involvement of technology serves to break down our invisible compartmental walls. Information, which would previously have been known in partial and restricted form by one person, is now stored in permanent and identifiable format by a second actor in the form of the form of the bank or credit card company involved. The point has been well made that "[t]he biggest threats to our privacy in a digital world come not from what we keep secret but from what we reveal willingly. We lose privacy in a digital world because it becomes cheap and easy to collate and transmit data, so that information you willingly gave a bank to get a mortgage suddenly ends up in the hands of a business rival or your ex-spouse's lawyer."[2]

During the 1960s and 1970s discussion of the dangers arising from computerised record keeping practices focused on the notion of a "Big Brother" style computer, a single vast filing system in which all information relating to every aspect of our lives would be held. In part, this reflected the view of technology at the time. It is a perhaps apocryphal tale that IBM estimated that 4 computers would suffice to satisfy the computing requirements of the United Kingdom, but it is certainly the case that when the major investigations of the Younger and Lindop Committees, on Privacy and Data Protection respectively discussed in Chapter 3, were being conducted in the 1970s computers were large and unwieldy objects. As was stated by Alan Westin, one of the early writers on the topic, "you do not find computers on street corners or in free nature, you find them in big powerful organisations" (Westin 1970).

The world, however, has moved on and at such a pace as to make liars of even the most prescient commentators. Computers are no longer monolithic machines which occupy the whole of a building. Today it is estimated that there are some 9,000,000 personal computers in use in the United Kingdom and if we take account of the further millions of electronic personal organisers it is clear that computers are now to be found on street corners, not least controlling the operation of traffic lights. A modern machine sitting on the corner of a small desk contains more computing power than one of the early monsters. A development of still greater significance has been the marriage between the computer and the telecommunications system. The consequence has been that computers control the telecommunications system which in turn provides a conduit through which computers can communicate with each other. More and more, the issue is not what information is held by a particular user, but what information which that user can access. In a sense the analogy may be between the books which are available on my desk as opposed to the books which are available on the shelves of a library of which I am a member. A critical difference is that the information will come to me rather than my having to visit the library and there is no danger that the book or information which I need will be on loan to another user. Possession, which is normally necessary for the use of a physical object, is a matter of little significance in an informational context.

In attempting to identify the implications arising from the application of information technology, a number of factors may be noted. First, more information is recorded about a particular transaction. That information may be readily accessible to a greater number of people. A further factor relates to the processing which may be conducted on the information and the actions which may be based upon the results obtained. At a simple level, most supermarkets use laser scanners at the checkouts. These identify the individual items which have been purchased. It is possible for a producer to make an agreement with the seller that whenever a competitor's products are recorded as having been purchased, a "money off" voucher will be issued to the customer, enticing her to transfer her business on the occasion of her next visit.

At this level of activity, data processing holds few implications for individuals *per se*. Analysis of purchasing patterns may result in some diminution of choice as slow moving items are discarded from stock. The issuing of vouchers tailored to the particular customer's purchases may have implications for competition between the producers involved. The next stage to be considered occurs where the individual is linked with particular transactions. In many situations, this linkage may not be made by a seller. In the event that the customer pays for the goods or services with a credit or debit card, the identifying data will be held by the supplier of the card although they will normally receive only limited information concerning the particular transaction. The shop will obtain details of the customer's name but not an address. Matters take on a different perspective when payment is made by means of an 'in-house' credit card and the creditor and the supplier become one and the same person.

All Information is Not the Same - or is it?

If the attempt is made to classify items of information concerning us, it might be possible to identify a model similar in concept to an onion. At the core of the model is the category of information which we regard as absolutely private. It might be regarded as the information that we would wish to share with no-one. Moving outwards, there may be a category of information that we regard as extremely sensitive. We may be willing to share it with a restricted number of people (or people falling within a specific category such as clerical or medical) but would not wish any wider dissemination. Next, we might identify information which we disseminate in the absence of any obligation of confidence and where the transfer occurs in some public forum although without the expectation that it will be recorded or subjected to a further transfer. An example might concern the purchase of items in a shop. Moving outwards, there is what can be regarded as our public persona. This encompasses items which, by law, are regarded as a matter of public record. Examples might include certificates of birth and marriage and entries on the electoral roll. Also included, although perhaps falling into a sub-category of their own, are items such as the list of shareholders in a public company. Finally, there may be identified categories of information which are put into the public domain on a voluntary basis. Entries in a telephone directory furnish a basic example but the scope of this category might expand to encompass advertising or the submission of letters or articles for publication in a newspaper or magazine.

Clearly, there can be no universal or exhaustive categorisation of the items of information which will fall into each of these categories. Individuals and societies may differ in their view as to what information is to be regarded as confidential. In the United Kingdom, for example, information held by the Inland Revenue is considered highly confidential, to the extent that sanctions may be imposed upon any employee who divulges information about a taxpayer's affairs. In Sweden by contrast, the tax returns submitted by individuals are regarded as a matter of public record[3]. Again, the terms of the British Official Secrets Acts may be compared with the freedom of information statutes enacted in countries such as Sweden and the United States. Regardless of the location of particular items of information, what may be identified is a move from a reluctance to have any form of dissemination, concern at the range of dissemination moving into a recognition that the information is available and a concern at the use to which it might be put. At this stage, it may be that privacy concerns are of very limited significance. There is an increasing tendency to place cameras in public areas. An individual who chooses to walk down a public street cannot have any realistic claim to privacy in that pursuit. The fact that movements are monitored by camera in no way changes the nature of the activity. The concern, if any, is not with the fact that information is obtained but with the use to which it may be put. At strongest, the argument may be advanced that conduct which is invasive of privacy may serve as the precursor or basis of other actions which may adversely affect other interests of the data subject.

As we move along the scale, account must increasingly be taken of the potential conflict between the wishes of the data subject and those of the other parties who may be involved. A claim to privacy will normally require to be balanced against another party's claim to seek information. This conflict is apparent from the provisions of the European Convention on Human Rights. Article 8 provides that "Everyone has the right to respect for his private and family life, his home and his correspondence" whilst Article 10 states that "Everyone has the right to freedom of expression. This right shall include freedom to hold opinions and to receive and impart information and ideas without interference by public authority and regardless of frontiers." This concluding sentence identifies a limiting factor which permeates all aspects of the Convention. It serves to confer rights upon individuals in the context of their relationships with public authorities. Its remit does not extend to the private sector.

Information Can Damage Your Health and Wealth

Information is a tool. It is today considered a truism to assert that "Information is power". In a very small number of cases, the mere fact that information is held may confer power upon the possessor. In most cases, as with other commodities, the power and the wealth arises from the use to which the commodity is put. Information is a more malleable commodity than coal, iron or any other physical product. Although swords may be beaten into ploughshares, the process is a difficult one and involves destruction of the original object. The uses to which information can be put are limited only by the imagination of its possessor and the same raw material may be used for an infinite number of purposes. In most cases, it may be assumed optimistically, the interests of the holder and the subject of personal data will coincide. What makes the attainment of any effective system of control difficult is the fact that the most mundane item of information may be used to the detriment of the subject, the most sensitive item to their benefit. Context is all important. Three incidents will be recounted below in which the use of recorded personal information played a critical role.

Population Registers

Prior to the Second World War, the Dutch government maintained an elaborate system of population registers (Hondius 1975). Most people would accept that Governments require to know a considerable amount of information about their citizens. As has been stated:

> Society seeks more services from both public and private organisations. From the government it expects social security, unemployment compensation ... All these increased services require that decisions be made (often instantly) and efficiently; information must be available to allow these decisions to be made. And such services require that records be kept - many records (Plishner 1981).

Included in the list of items of information held in the present case was a statement as to the religious affiliation of the citizens. The justification for holding such information might appear tenuous but, given the traditional involvement of religious organisations in the fields of health care and education, could be considered reasonable. The danger in the system manifested itself when the German army invaded Holland during the Second World War, captured the Registers and thereby a list of the name and address of every Jew in the country.

An Unhappy Birthday

Few people would regard details of their date of birth as being of any practical sensitivity. In the United States during the 1960s a chain of ice cream parlours ran a promotional campaign targeted at its teenage customers. In return for details of the customer's date of birth, the company undertook to send a card and a voucher for a free ice cream on the eighteenth birthday. For thousands of teenagers, the offer was too good to miss. At the time in question, reaching one's eighteenth birthday signified more than just an entitlement to a free ice cream. The Vietnam war was in progress and those attaining eighteen years of age were obliged to register for compulsory military service. Evasion was widespread and the military authorities took extensive measures to identify those involved. As part of this endeavour, they sought and obtained the ice cream parlour's records (10 *Transnational Data Report* 25).

Sign Here

A final incident occurred in the United Kingdom during the passage of the measure that was to become the Abolition of Domestic Rates (Scotland) Act 1988. This statute, which introduced the system of community charges (poll tax) prompted considerable opposition and a number of petitions were presented to Parliament. Faced with criticism that the Government were taking inadequate account of these petitions, the response was made by the Minister of State that the list of names and addresses contained therein "could be a useful source of information for the Community Charge Registration Officer" (i.e. be used to track down those who had evaded the requirement to register as liable to pay the charge). Asked to confirm that "from now on the names and addresses on petitions will be used for the purpose of gathering the poll tax", the response was "That is broadly what I suggested" (130 *Official Report (House of Commons)* 29 March 1988: col 851).

Towards Some Conclusions?

A number of observations may be made concerning the above incidents. First, it may be noted that the word computer is nowhere used. Indeed, the most lethal incident preceded the machine's invention. The danger of informational abuse did not await the computer. The Dutch example serves to illustrate a further point. No legal system can provide absolute security against external threats. Abstinence from record keeping is the only certain safeguard. Although this will seldom be a practical or desirable option, an assessment requires to be made of the level of risk and of any security measures which may be available. Any record keeping involves the subject giving a hostage to fortune.

The second example serves to raise the issue which is central to much of the debate in the area. Put simply, where does the right lie? Certainly, information supplied for one purpose was put to another use, but the obligation to register for military service was prescribed by law. The military authorities were attempting to enforce the law whilst the unregistered ice cream addicts were in breach of it. Such an analysis may be considered unduly simplistic. Only a proportion of those whose details were disclosed would have been in breach of the law. The argument is often heard: "If you have done nothing wrong then you have nothing to hide". The corollary may be that "If I have done nothing wrong, what right have others to interfere?" The issue is one which has been exacerbated by the computer. It is possible to store vast amounts of data in a physically tiny space. Parkinson's law tells us that work expands to fill the time available for its completion. It appears equally true that the need to store information expands in line with any increase in storage capacity. Information is sought and retained on the many against the eventuality that it may be used against the few.

The final example cited raises further complex issues. Again, there might be a conflict between the interests of law enforcement and the individual's claim "to be let alone". Again, there is a situation where information supplied for one purpose is used for another. In the United States example, if the question were posed "What would the respondents to the promotional campaign have done had they known that their involvement would be recorded and used against them?", the answer is obvious. A reluctance to respond to promotional campaigns might be regarded as a matter of little significance. The consequences of a similar response in the United Kingdom example might be considered more serious. It is apposite to make reference to a recent decision of the German Constitutional Court in which the tribunal was asked to rule on the constitutionality of a statute prescribing the information which was to be supplied by citizens in connection with a national census and the uses to which this information might be put. The possibilities of data transfer led to the statute being struck down as unconstitutional. Whilst the Court recognised the legitimate need of the state to gather information about its citizens, it held that:

> The possibilities of inspection and of gaining influence have increased to a degree hitherto unknown and may influence the individual's behaviour by the psychological pressure exerted by public interest ... if someone cannot predict with sufficient certainty which information about himself in certain areas is known to his social milieu, and cannot estimate sufficiently the knowledge of parties to whom communication may possibly be made, he is crucially inhibited in his freedom to plan or to decide freely and without being subject to any pressure/influence. (5 Human Rights Law Journal (1984) 94)

The Court went on to cite a reluctance to participate in a "citizens initiative" as a specific illustration of the undesirable consequences which might flow from such informational uncertainty. It has indeed been suggested that developments in data processing make the concept of a universal census obsolete. The information required, it is argued, can be obtained through more selective techniques similar to those used in opinion polls. Such a step has been taken in Norway.

The previous sections have sought to identify some of the dangers facing individuals as a result of actions being based upon recorded information. The notion of recording personal information is not new. The twelfth-century Domesday Book is one of the best known collections of information whilst a census is integral to the Gospel stories . What is novel about the modern era is the degree to which decisions and actions are based upon reference to recorded information as opposed to any form of personal knowledge or individual assessment. In previous generations, an individual wishing to secure a bank loan would have to endure an interview with a bank manager who would base a decision in part upon his or her subjective assessment of the applicant's character perhaps coupled with some personal knowledge of the state of the latter's finances. Today, a similar information is likely to be made in writing with the decision being based upon recorded information held either by the potential creditor or by a credit reference agency. In other cases, the use of credit scoring techniques may remove almost all trace of individual judgment from the exercise. Based upon an assessment of many thousands of credit transactions, credit scoring techniques seek to ascertain and weight the factors which may influence the likelihood of a debtor making full repayment. Factors such as age, occupation, marital status, income, can all be taken into account together with the applicants status as a tenant, lodger or home-owner. Point-age values are allocated to the various items of information. The task for the potential creditor is to add up the various elements and consult a table which indicates the statistically probability of default associated with various values. It may be, for example, that a score of 20 points equates to a 5% risk of default. If the score rises to 25 points, the risk of default may drop to 3%. Essentially, the creditor may choose what degree of risk it is willing to accept. No account need be taken of the particular circumstances of the applicant.

If record keeping has been present for centuries, the development of the computer and the nature of the operations associated with it open the way to new forms of behaviour. More information can be held in a given space. To give a simple example. A compact disk - which is not a particularly efficient storage device - can hold 650 mega bytes of data. The text of this work occupies about half a megabyte. A single disk could hold 1,300 copies of this work. About 20 metres of shelving would be required to hold that amount of paper. Beyond the issue of storage capacity, the linkage between the computer and the telephone referred to earlier allows data to be entered and retrieved from many different places. A travel agent, for example, will be able to access the computerised reservation system of an airline or holiday company, discover the availability of seats or holidays and make a booking. The geographical location of the travel agent and the computer system is almost irrelevant.

The ease with which data may be transmitted and accessed introduces a significant international dimension to the topic. Assuming that the necessary communications facilities are built into the system, data held anywhere in the world can be accessed from anywhere else using the normal telephone system. One example can be seen in the computerised legal retrieval system *Lexis*. This contains a substantial amount of English and Scottish legal materials and is widely used by legal practitioners. The data base is physically located in Ohio in the United States. Every use of the system from the United Kingdom involves an international or transnational data flow. In this context the issues raised affect governments and concerns of national sovereignty to a greater extent than they do individual rights[4].

A further aspect of computer operations to be considered concerns the nature of the processing which may be undertaken. In the 1975 White Paper, *Computers and Privacy* (Cmnd 6353) it was asserted that computers "make it practicable for data to be combined in ways which might not otherwise be practicable". The key word in this phrase is "practicable" If a human were to be given a telephone number and a telephone directory and asked to find the name and address associated with the number it would be possible for her to discover the necessary linkage. Such a task would involve no intellectual effort but few people would regard it as a practical undertaking. Such processing involving a mixture of searching and comparison would be well suited for a computer and even a small machine could be programmed toobtain the information in a matter of seconds.

The conclusion at this stage may be that to an increasing extent decisions affecting significant aspects of our lives and fortunes are made on the basis of recorded information. The practices make new facilities and services available and by removing elements of subjectivity from the decision-making process may avoid the effects of bias and prejudice. The point has been made on a number of occasions that information is to be considered a commodity. As with all other commodities it may be used in ways which are harmful. Over the past 25 years, the concept of data protection has become recognised as a major component of the legal response to the dangers of informational misuse. The following chapter will examine the evolution of data protection paying specific and critical attention to the features of the United Kingdom's Data Protection Act 1984. As this statute enters its second decade, the chapter will conclude with an examination of the proposed European Directive on data protection, the enactment of which would require the making of significant changes to the existing regime.

Chapter Three

Elements of Data Protection

The Move to Legislation

In 1969 the Data Surveillance Bill was introduced in the House of Commons by Kenneth Baker MP. This proposal, in common with a number of other Private Members' Bills introduced during the 1970s and early 1980s never appeared likely to reach the statute book. Had its fate been different, the United Kingdom would have been the first country in the world to enact data protection legislation. In the event, that honour went to Germany where the state of Hesse enacted legislation in 1970. Sweden followed with the first national statute in 1973 whilst United Kingdom legislation, in the form of the Data Protection Act, did not reach the statute book until 1984.

The fact that legislation appeared first in Germany and Sweden might be explained by differing historical factors. In Germany, awareness from the time of the Nazi era of the dangers arising from personal records was a major factor behind the decision to legislate in the early stages of the computer revolution. Indeed, legislative initiatives have continued in Germany. In 1986 the Hessian legislature enacted its third data protection statute. A number of other states have also legislated in the field whilst two national statutes have been enacted in 1974 and 1990. If the German legislation can be seen as based upon a recognition of the need to control the activities of data users, the Swedish legislation fell naturally into a tradition of openness in record keeping and the operation of principles of subject access. The lengthy struggle for the enactment of data protection legislation in the United Kingdom, coupled with problems encountered in the operation of the statute, might suggest that the concept fits uneasily into the political and legal landscape.

Within the United Kingdom the data protection tide ebbed and flowed during the 1970s. In 1972 the Committee on Privacy - which had been appointed by the Government in 1970 in return for the dropping of a well supported but unwelcome (to the government) private members' bill seeking to establish a statutory right to privacy - devoted a chapter of its report to the privacy implications arising from computer use. The Committee, whose remit was confined to the private sector[1], identified the potential dangers discussed in the previous chapter but rejected the call for legislative intervention, concluding that these could be averted by compliance with a voluntary code containing ten principles. The view that legislation was unnecessary lasted only until 1975 when a White Paper was published entitled *Computers and Privacy*. This announced that "In the Government's view the time has come when those who use computers to handle personal information can no longer remain the sole judges of whether their own systems adequately safeguard privacy" (DTI 1975: para 30). An intention to legislate was announced and a further committee, the Committee on Data Protection, appointed to advise the Government on the precise form that such a statute should take.

The Committee's report was published in 1978. It joined the Committee on Privacy in recommending that users should comply with a number of data protection principles although the merging of a number of the earlier formulations reduced the total number to seven. Recognising that general statements of principle would require to be interpreted in the context of specific applications and users, it was recommended that the principles should be supplemented by some 50 statutory codes of practice. Compliance would be secured through the appointment of a two-tiered supervisory agency. A full-time Data Protection Executive would oversee the day to day functioning of the legislation whilst a Data Protection Authority - with a membership selected as representative of the various interests involved in data processing - would assume executive responsibility for the new regime.

The report of the Committee on Data Protection is a voluminous document extending to 460 pages. As such, it is perhaps the most extensive study of the issues involved ever conducted. Its impact, however, on subsequent legislative developments has been minimal. In a White Paper published on the topic in 1982, the Committee's report was considered to constitute only "very helpful background information". More respect was afforded to the report of the Committee on Privacy which devoted only 15 pages to the implications of computerisation; the Home Secretary stating in answer to a Parliamentary question that "[t]he Government accepts as a starting point the recommendations of the [Committee on Privacy] ... Our intention is that the legislation should incorporate and so far as possible give effect to these principles" (Official Report (House of Commons) 19 March 1981, Col 161).

International Initiatives

Although deference was shown to the work of the Committee on Privacy, the fact that a Data Protection Bill was introduced in 1982 undoubtedly owed more to international developments and concern for the economic interests of United Kingdom-based data users than for the interests of individual data subjects.

Following the German and Swedish initiatives, data protection statutes mushroomed throughout western Europe. As states introduced controls over data processing operations located within their own territories, so concern mounted at the possible establishment of data havens. In the same way that funds might be transferred out of one state into another with a more lenient tax regime, so data users might be tempted to transfer data abroad in order to engage in processing which would be unlawful under their national regime.

Apart from the possible circumvention of national laws, there was also a concern that the absence of data protection statutes in countries such as the United Kingdom might constitute a factor persuading multi-national undertakings to locate investment in a jurisdiction which would impose no controls over their data processing operations.

The negotiation and introduction of the Council of Europe Convention on the Automated Processing of Personal Data can be identified as a response to these concerns. The Convention lays down standards to be observed in national laws and binds signatories to refrain from erecting any barriers to the transfer of personal data to another signatory state on the ground of protecting individual privacy. The unwritten threat was that sanctions might be imposed against transfers to non-signatory states and, indeed, in the lead up to the enactment of the Data Protection Act, incidents were recounted of United Kingdom-based firms losing contracts because of a refusal by national data protection authorities in France and Sweden to sanction the transfer of personal data.

The entry into force of the Council of Europe convention brought pressure from representatives of industry for legislation to be introduced enabling the United Kingdom to sign and ratify the instrument. These commercial pressures succeeded where civil libertarian concerns had failed. A Data Protection Bill was introduced into the House of Lords in 1982 only to be lost with the dissolution of Parliament prior to a general election in 1983. The Bill was reintroduced in the autumn of 1983 and ultimately received the Royal Assent in 1984.

One of the leading actors in the data protection field, Professor Spiro Simitis, formerly Data Protection Commissioner in Hesse, has commented that data protection statutes have an effective life span of seven years. After this, it is argued, changes in technology and practices render them obsolete. By this standard, the Data Protection Act's retirement is somewhat overdue. Paradoxically, given that it was enacted because of external influences, international factors are now hindering its amendment. In 1989 the Data Protection Registrar conducted a consultation exercise and published proposals for reform of the legislation. In 1990 proposals for a European Directive were published. It was originally envisaged that the proposals would be enacted and implemented in Member States by January 1993. Enactment of the Directive in anything like the form proposed would require significant amendment to the Data Protection Act and there has been an understandable reluctance to make what could be short lived amendments whilst the shape and future of the European proposals remained uncertain. It would now appear that the dates for enactment and implementation have slipped from 1995 to 1997 and the Registrar has indicated that any further slippage in the timetable would make independent domestic reform a matter of some urgency.

Basic Definitions

The criterion for the Act's application is that a data user[2] should process personal data relating to one or more data subjects. In common with almost all European data protection regimes, the Act establishes an independent supervisory authority in the form of the Data Protection Registrar. It is further provided that the Registrar is to be assisted by a Deputy Registrar and an unspecified number of other staff to be appointed by the Registrar with the consent of the Treasury. At present some 90 permanent staff are so employed. Any decisions made by the Registrar which affect a data user adversely may be appealed to a Data Protection Tribunal consisting of a legally qualified chairman and deputy chairmen and representatives of data users and data subjects. All data users are obliged to register details of their activities, the information being entered onto the Data Protection Register. Subsequent to registration, users are required to ensure that their processing activities conform with eight data protection principles and face a variety of administrative, civil or even criminal sanctions in the event of any failure.

There is no doubt that the Data Protection Act is intended to regulate electronic or computerised data processing. Perhaps wisely, the Act, in common with virtually all statutory interventions in the computer-related field, eschews any definition of "computer" and indeed the word itself appears only in a peripheral context. Instead the legislation talks in terms of the processing of personal data by "equipment operating automatically in response to instructions given for that purpose" (section 1(2)). This definition certainly encompasses all computer applications. In the 1970s and even in the early 1980s this would have made up a comparatively small constituency. Reference has previously been made to the 9,000,000 personal computers in use in the United Kingdom. All of these, plus the vast number of electronic personal organisers possessed by every would-be entrepreneur or manager, are eminently capable of processing personal data. The Data Protection Act's definition is even sufficiently broad to include a number of non-computer-related functions. Many homes possess a form of telephone directory where names and numbers are written on cards stored in alphabetical order and the act of depressing a key on the outer surface causes the directory to open at the appropriate place. Such a method of operation will constitute processing under the statutory definition.

The legislation does provide for a number of operations and users to enjoy total or partial exemption. Most significantly in numerical terms, those processing only for social or domestic purposes will incur no obligations under the Act. A number of other exemptions are provided for in the legislation although these are hedged with so many conditions and provisos that the Registrar has expressed the view that they are unlikely to benefit any but the smallest users. In principle, the fact that millions of persons and organisations are subject to legislation poses no difficulties. What makes the effect on the data protection regime problematic is the requirement imposed upon all data users to register details of their activities with the Data Protection Registrar and pay a fee of £75 (a fee raised in stages from the initial £26) for a registration valid for three years. Although it was argued by the Government that the introduction of a system of near universal registration was necessary in order to conform with the requirement of the Convention, it is now generally recognised that this is not the case and it would suffice to impose on at least smaller-scale data users a requirement that they comply with the substantive provisions of the legislation.

Faced with a situation where the cost of registration may exceed that of the equipment involved, it is not surprising that evasion has been widespread. As last reported, the Data Protection Register contains 188,766 entries. An unregistered user who processes personal data will commit a criminal offence. Although it is impossible to ascertain the exact number of those who are liable to register under the Act there can be no doubt that a very significant number of data users have failed to register. To mid-1994, 161 data users have been prosecuted for failure to register. Organisations involved include Levi Strauss Jeans, the *Spectator* magazine and the International Society for Krishna Consciousness. A cynic might query whether the activities of organisations such as these are likely to pose significant threats to individual rights. Although the widespread evasion of the registration requirement may not pose significant threats to individuals, knowledge of its occurrence must serve to bring the legislation into a measure of disrepute. The Registrar's review of the legislation advocated considerable pruning of the registration requirements so as to remove 90% of those currently on the Register although this would have the effect of increasing very significantly the fees charged to his remaining clients.

A more controversial exemption excludes any data processing which is conducted in connection with national security. A certificate by a Minister to this effect is conclusive evidence on the point (section 27). In line with traditional practice, this term is not defined and there may be difficulty in determining where national security ends and policing - which is covered by the legislation albeit subject to some exceptions - begins. The recent dispute between the Special Branch and MI5 over which organisation should enjoy primacy in the campaign against the activities of the IRA in mainland Britain indicates how blurred may be the boundary between the two activities. For the purposes of the Data Protection Act, of course, it is the activity rather than the organisation which is important but a further complicating factor is that the ministerial certificates referred to above are not issued in advance but will only be provided in the event that the Registrar indicates an intention to take any action against a particular user

The approach adopted in the United Kingdom legislation may not conform with the requirements of the European Convention. Although this recognises the special requirements of national security, it sanctions only such "derogation" as "constitutes a necessary measure in a democratic society" (Article 9(2)). The same formulation is found in the European Convention of Human Rights and case law under this instrument indicates that total exclusion will seldom be an acceptable option. In a number of other signatory states, procedures have been adopted whereby national security data is exempted from aspects of the legislation, especially those concerned with conferring access rights upon data subjects, but remain subject to the scrutiny of the supervisory agency. By eschewing such an option the United Kingdom authorities may have failed to comply with their Treaty obligations although the data processing Convention, unlike its human rights predecessor, makes no provision for national actions to be challenged before the Commission and Court of Human Rights.

Personal Data and Data Processing

Personal data is defined as any data relating to a living, identifiable individual. It is provided further that this includes any statements of opinion which may be recorded concerning the data subject but excludes any statement of the intentions which the user may hold relating to the subject (section 1(3)).

The question whether a subject is alive or dead may be expected to pose few problems but the remaining aspects of the definition are fraught with problems. The opinion/intention distinction in the data protection field has proved almost as impenetrable as the idea/expression dichotomy in the copyright arena. The explanation put forward by the government at the time of the Act's passage was that statements of intention belonged to the responsible user rather than to the subject. This view is not without merit but it is difficult to see how any different conclusion can be drawn concerning opinions. Even the Data Protection Registrar commented in his review of the Act in 1989 that "it is not at all clear what the distinction is between an opinion and an intention" and has recommended its repeal. Enactment and implementation of the proposed European Union Directive would have this effect in bringing all information relating to an individual within the scope of the legislation.

Another problematic issue concerns the question when individuals may be considered identifiable. Clearly this must be the case if they are referred to by name. Names, however, are an inefficient form of identifier. A glance at any telephone directory will reveal the number of people who share the same or a similar name. Even a single person may be referred to in a variety of ways using various combinations of names and initials. It is also possible that individuals may, quite lawfully, determine to change their name. Numbers provide a more accurate form of identifier. In some countries individuals are allocated a personal identification number at birth, this number being used throughout the individual's life. In terms of administrative efficiency, such a system offers many advantages. It also offers the prospect of very efficient correlation of information held by a number of parties and in a number of countries proposals for the introduction of such a system have been dropped following public criticism of the adverse implications for individual privacy. No single system of personal identifiers operates in the United Kingdom, but there is no doubt that where information is held by reference to bank account numbers, national insurance numbers or any other form of identifier, the Act will apply. The question whether an individual is to be considered identifiable is also linked to the definition of processing. Here the Act refers to activities involving "amending, augmenting, deleting or re-arranging the data or extracting the information constituting the data and, in the case of personal data, means performing any of those operations by reference to the data subject" (section 1(7)).

The operations defined above are basic computing functions and it is doubted whether any act involving a computer will not constitute processing. The limiting factor is that the processing must be conducted "by reference to the data subject". A user can hold an unlimited amount of personal data without the legislation coming into play. An example might concern the storage of copies of newspapers on electronic format. Any issue of a newspaper will contain a significant amount of personal data. The act of loading a copy onto a data base will not be conducted by reference to any particular data subject and so will not fall within the scope of the Act. Assuming, however, that the data base permits a user to search by reference to names so that it is possible to retrieve all stories relating to a particular individual, processing as defined in the Data Protection Act will occur. Use of a computerised legal retrieval service which permits a user to search by reference to the names of parties involved in cases will involve processing.

Beyond the situation where information is sought about one individual, where data is processed by reference to some form of identifier, e.g. all people born in the year 1955, processing will be assumed to have taken place with reference to each individual whose data falls within the search parameters. In the first cases dealt with by the Data Protection Tribunal, the processing operations of credit reference agencies were challenged by the Registrar. Credit reference agencies have traditionally retrieved data by reference to address rather than by name. This form of processing might well retrieve information on a number of past and present residents. Although almost every other aspect of the Registrar's actions were challenged before the Tribunal, the fact that processing of personal data had taken place was not in dispute.

The Data Protection Principles

The major continuing duty imposed on the Registrar is to ensure that users comply with eight data protection principles. These require that:

1. The information to be contained in personal data shall be obtained, and personal data shall be processed, fairly and lawfully.
2. Personal data shall only be held for one or more specified and lawful purposes.
3. Personal data held for any purpose or purposes shall not be used or disclosed in any manner incompatible with that purpose or those purposes.
4. Personal data held for any purpose or purposes shall be adequate, relevant and not excessive in relation to that purpose or those purposes.
5. Personal data shall be accurate and, where necessary, kept up to date.
6. Personal data held for any purpose or purposes shall not be kept for longer than is necessary for that purpose or those purposes.
7. An individual shall be entitled -

(a)   at reasonable intervals and without undue delay or expense -
(i)   to be informed by any data user whether he holds personal data of which that individual is the subject; and
(ii)   to access to any such data held by a data user; and
(b)   where appropriate, to have such data corrected or erased.
8.   Appropriate security precautions shall be taken against unauthorised access to, or alteration, disclosure or destruction of, personal data and against accidental loss or destruction of personal data (schedule 1).

A number of the principles are supplemented by further provisions within the body of the statute. It may be a criticism of the Act that in the majority of instances this takes the form of providing for exceptions from their application.

As stated above, failure by a user to comply with the principles may meet with a variety of consequences. In all cases, breach may result in the Data Protection Registrar taking action against the user. This will normally take the form of service of an enforcement notice (section 10). Such a notice may be either positive or negative in its terms, instructing the user to act or desist from acting in specified ways. Failure to comply with an enforcement notice will constitute a criminal offence and may also expose the user to the Registrar's ultimate sanction in the form of service of a de-registration notice. As the name suggests, this expunges the user's entry from the Data Protection Register rendering continued processing of personal data unlawful (section 11).

The data protection principles serve as a technical equivalent to the Ten Commandments in providing provide general statements of acceptable computer practice. A number of these might be regarded as self-evident. It would be a masochistic data user who deliberately held inaccurate or out-of-date data. In common with all generalities, the data protection principles will require to be interpreted in the context of particular forms of data processing. In a number of cases codes of practice have been promulgated by trade or professional associations providing interpretative guidance in the context of particular applications. Such codes are purely voluntary documents although the fact of compliance or non-compliance with a relevant code may have evidentiary value in any dispute concerning the acceptability of a user's behaviour.

In terms of altering the behaviour of data users, three aspects may be identified as worthy of more detailed consideration. The logical starting point concerns the manner in which data is acquired, this is followed by issues concerning the permitted use and disclosure of data and, finally, attention must be paid to the operation of and exceptions to the subject access provisions.

Acquisition of Data

The first data protection principle requires that data be obtained and processed fairly and lawfully. A significant exception to the application of this principle occurs when data is obtained in connection with the prevention or detection of crime, the apprehension or prosecution of offenders or the collection or assessment of any tax or duty; it being provided that the Registrar may take no action against the user on the basis of a breach of the first principle where this would be likely to prejudice the attainment of the purpose in question (section 28(4)). The justification put forward for the exemption is that the nature of policing activities entails that data may be received which has been acquired in what may be regarded as dubious circumstances. Whilst this view has considerable merit, it may be that the matter would be dealt with better by providing a detailed definition of the principle than by excluding its operation, especially for the situations where data was obtained unlawfully. The breadth of the exception is rendered more objectionable by the fact that registration in connection with policing purposes is not restricted to police forces. Although anyone obtaining information unlawfully may face sanctions in respect of this, denying the Registrar the discretion to act in such cases diminishes the role and status of the Data Protection Act.

Another aspect of fair obtaining relates to the fourth data protection principle which requires that the data held should not be excessive in relation to the purpose for which it is held. As has been stated previously, the enhanced storage potential created by the computer may tempt users to collect as much information as possible against the eventuality that they may find use for it. The fourth principle should cause them to guard against this temptation. An illustration of its operation can be taken from the decisions of the Data Protection Tribunal in a number of cases concerned with the operation of the Community Charge (*Community Charge Registration Officer of Runnymede Borough Council v Data Protection Registrar, Community Charge Registration Officer of South Northamptonshire District Council v Data Protection Registrar, Community Charge Registration Officer of Harrow Borough Council v Data Protection Registrar and the Community Charge Registration Officer of Rhondda Borough Council v Data Protection Registrar*). A key feature of the system involved the compilation of registers of those liable to pay the tax. As a single charge was levied upon all taxpayers, the information required by statute to be held on the registers was limited to a record of the taxpayer's name and address. A number of authorities sought to include additional items of information on their computerised registers. This resulted in the service by the Data Protection Registrar of a number of enforcement notices. These notices were upheld by the Tribunal. Examples of categories of information whose acquisition and storage was held to be unlawful included dates of birth and the kind of property where the taxpayer was resident. Significantly, the fact that taxpayers - who supplied the information making up the registers - were informed in a number of cases that they were not required to supply additional items of information was not regarded as providing any form of defence.

Use and Disclosure of Data

Beyond controlling the manner in which information is obtained, the data protection principles require that processing be conducted fairly and lawfully. Again, it is the criterion of fairness which gives rise to most problems. Action taken by the Registrar against the major credit reference agencies alleging breaches of this principle resulted in the first cases to be heard by the Data Protection Tribunal.

The function of a credit reference agency is to acquire information relevant to a determination of an individual's credit worthiness and to make this available to those who are considering extending credit facilities to that person. The nature of the agencies' operations was that information was recorded by reference to address rather than to an individual's name. Extracting information on this basis in the context of a credit application made by one individual would also retrieve information about any other persons who were or had been resident at the address. The Registrar alleged that this form of processing contravened the first data protection principle and served an enforcement notice upon each of the four major credit reference agencies involved requiring cessation of the practice.

Although all the agencies operated in a similar fashion, their appeals were heard separately before the Tribunal with different issues being raised (and in large part rejected) in each case (*CCN Systems v Data Protection Registrar, Infolink Ltd v Data Protection Registrar, Equifax Europe Ltd v Data Protection Registrar and Credit* and *Data Marketing Services Ltd v Data Protection Registrar*). An initial claim was that the practice of retrieving information by reference to address was justifiable as there was a statistical correlation between past defaults and the likelihood that another person resident at the same address would act in like fashion. This claim did not find favour with the Tribunal. Although it accepted that such a correlation might exist at the general level, it had no predictive value in respect of the particular individual whose credit application was being considered. A further argument sought to impose limits on the definition of processing as contained in the Act. This referred to the "amending, augmenting, deleting or re-arranging the data or extracting the information constituting the data". The first data protection principle would be infringed if processing was unfair. The principle, it was argued made no reference to the use to which the data was put but stopped at the stage of its extraction. The extraction of data was a neutral process and could not, it was submitted, be stigmatised as unfair. Such an interpretation would serve to rob the first principle of much of its effect. The Tribunal were of a different opinion. Although the operation of computers might be value free, the machines could function only in accordance with their programs. These reflected the intentions of the operators[3], and it was these which required to be the subject of the Tribunal's determination of fairness.

One final point deserves mention concerning the decisions in these cases. The argument was advanced that prohibiting the practice of extracting third party information would result in an increase in the level of bad debt or, perhaps, in the denial of credit to persons who might otherwise have been accepted. This it was argued would itself result in unfairness. Whilst recognising that credit reference agencies did provide a valuable service to the credit industry, the purpose of the Data Protection Act was to safeguard the interests of individual data subjects. Considerations of the greater good could not prevail over those of the individual. Clearly such an approach must have its limits; otherwise individuals with a poor credit history might claim that it was against their interests that the information should be recorded and processed. What the Tribunal's decision does signify is that processing which is considered to have the potential of unfairness as regards the legitimate interests of a data subject will not be permitted on the basis that it offers benefits to the user.

In other situations the major area of concern relates to the issue whether an individual has been informed of the use to which information will be put. This issue is related closely to that of the manner in which information is obtained. In many instances, the information will be supplied by the data subject concerned on a voluntary basis. A typical example might see the individual giving details of name and address when ordering goods or services by post. Such details are necessary if the purpose of the transaction is to be attained. If the information is used only for this purpose, no difficulties will arise. In many cases, however, the user will wish to maintain a record of the subject's details on a mailing list. It may also be envisaged that access to the mailing list will be granted to other users. Here information which has been supplied freely for one use is being put to another use. In the case of *Innovations Ltd v Data Protection Registrar* (1993: summarised in the Tenth Report of the Data Protection Registrar, 32), the Data Protection Tribunal upheld the Registrar's contention that a failure to inform mail order customers of the fact that their details might be supplied to other companies at the time the data was first collected constituted a breach of the first data protection principle.

The starting point for consideration of the controls over the disclosure of data to third parties is the third data protection principle which provides that:

> Personal data held for any purpose or purposes shall not be used or disclosed in any manner incompatible with that purpose or those purposes.

This principle receives considerable expansion in the body of the statute. In every case, this takes the form of providing exemptions from its application, an approach which incurred the displeasure of Sir Norman Lindop, the Chairman of the Committee on Data Protection who was moved to write a letter to *The Times* complaining that the legislation "perpetrated a fraud on the public". The basis for this accusation was that whilst the third principle proclaimed the notion that data could only be disclosed in accordance with the terms of the user's entry on the Register, the exemption provided for contrary and secretive disclosures.

In every case where the Act makes provision for disclosures outwith the scope of the user's entry on the Register, there can be little dispute that some provision may be necessary. Thus it is provided that the principle is not to apply where disclosure is made for the purpose of the prevention or detection of crime, the apprehension or prosecution of offenders or the collection or assessment of any tax or duty and in circumstances where a failure to disclose it likely to prejudice the attainment of the purpose specified (section 28(1)). Instances may be identified readily where the operation of an exemption would be eminently justified. Few users might be expected to identify the police authorities as likely recipients of their data when drawing up their Register entry. In the event, however, that a fraud was perpetrated on the user, the police might require to obtain access to the user's computer system and to the personal data held therein in the course of their investigations. In the absence of any statutory exemption, such an act would infringe the terms of the user's registration. Where the provisions can fairly be criticised is in respect of their breadth - there is no requirement that the criminal offence be of any order of magnitude, so that an investigation into non-payment of a parking fine would be treated in the same vein as a murder inquiry. Particular concern might be expressed in respect of the crime prevention exception. Crime prevention is a nebulous concept and it is difficult to identify any item of data which could not be regarded as possessing some relevance to this topic. Although it is the case that the test whether a disclosure is justified has a second element - that a failure to disclose would prejudice the attainment of the specified purpose - there is again no requirement that there be any significant degree of impairment.

Beyond the substantive concerns regarding the scope of the exemptions, the legislation contains no procedural safeguards whatsoever. A request for a disclosure may be made by the most junior police officer and responded to by the most junior member of the data user's staff. Although either or both of the actors may face internal disciplinary sanctions the data users will have nothing to fear from the Data Protection Act. Further, there is no requirement that any record be kept of the fact that disclosure has been sought and granted and no requirement that the Registrar, or anyone else, be informed of what has occurred.

A variety of other exemptions are provided for in the legislation. In terms of their area of application, these are less controversial that those discussed above although in a number of cases the scope of the provision is obscure. The non-disclosure principle will not apply where the disclosure is made for the purpose of obtaining legal advice or where the disclosure is required by order of a court. Disclosure may also be made when it is urgently required to safeguard the health of the data subject or of any other person.

Subject Access

From the individual's perspective, the subject access provisions constitute the most significant innovation in the legislation. Although a number of criticisms may be made of the manner in which the terms of the seventh data protection principle have been implemented in the body of the statute, the fact remains that the passage of the Act marked a very significant extension to the right of individuals to secure access to personal data.

A data user is obliged to respond only to requests which are received in writing and which provide such information as may reasonably be required to confirm the identity of the applicant and to permit the user to locate any relevant data (Section 21). It is, of course only the data subject or a person authorised to act on their behalf who lawfully may exercise the right of access. A user who discloses data to anyone other than the subject will breach the non-disclosure principle. Given this possibility, it may not be unreasonable for a user to seek additional items of information. If the subject has been allocated some form of identification number by the user, provision of this information may avoid any confusion with data relating to other subjects sharing the same name as the applicant. It may be difficult to distinguish, however, between a request by the user for further information designed to elicit information in order to ensure that the enquiring subject receives all relevant data (and none pertaining to a third party) and one which is intended to cause delay and perhaps to dissuade the applicant from pursuing a request.

A further aspect of subject access is the question of cost. The seventh principle states that a subject is to be entitled to access at a reasonable cost. When the Act's access provisions became operative in 1986, it was provided that a user would be entitled to require payment of a fee of up to £10. This fee was significantly higher than that suggested by the Registrar and also significantly greater than the fee of £1 pertaining to a request for access to data held by a credit reference agency under the similar provisions of the Consumer Credit Act 1974. The ten-fold difference in fee levels was justified at the time on the basis that credit reference agencies structured their data in such a way as to facilitate retrieval by reference to the individual whilst many users operating under the auspices of the Data Protection Act might not routinely extract information in this way. An example might concern the controller of a mailing list. As the cases brought before the Data Protection Tribunal indicate, this view of the nature of credit reference agencies' operations may have been misguided. Although the fee has not been increased in line with subsequent inflation, it continues to represent a major barrier to access. The problem may be compounded by the fact that many users have divided their data holdings into separate entries on the Register. It may be that a number of the entries might contain information relating to a particular subject and in such an event the user will be able to require a separate fee in respect of each file searched. The fee will be payable even if a particular file contains no information on the subject.

Having received a valid request for access, a user is normally obliged to supply the subject with a copy of their personal data within 40 days. An extension may be sought from the Registrar if the circumstances of a particular case justify delay. Research conducted into the operation of the Act would suggest that a significant number of users fail to respond to access requests within the permitted period.

In responding to a request for access, the data which must be supplied to the subject is that which was held at the date the access request was received by the user. This is subject to a partial exception where the data is subjected to routine processing between the date of receipt and the date when the requisite copy is taken. An example might concern transactions relating to a subject's bank account where sums may routinely be credited and debited on a daily basis. The data is to be supplied to the subject in writing together with an explanation of any terms or codes used in the record whose meaning might not readily be apparent.

The operation of the subject access principle is subject to one general and to a number of sectoral exceptions. As with the exceptions to the non-disclosure principle, whilst the need for some exceptional provisions will be accepted by most people, there is scope for concern at the manner in which they have been implemented.

The general exception to the access right occurs where the data concerned relates to a third party. In principle, this approach must be regarded as correct. The third party is as entitled to have his or her data protected as is the enquiring data subject to access. Unless the third party has consented to the disclosure, the user will breach the third data protection principle should the information be disclosed to anyone else. In many instances, of course, the data concerning two or more parties may be tightly linked. A typical situation will arise where the third party has served as the source of information about the data subject.

The Act contains a number of provisions which are designed to allow a satisfactory compromise to be reached between the competing claims of access and non-disclosure. Users are instructed that all practical steps are to be taken to suppress the third party's identity thereby allowing the remainder of the data to be supplied to the subject. One instance has been reported where a data subject sought access to records relating to a bank account held jointly with a partner. The transcript supplied had all references to the partner's name and transactions blanked out. Whilst showing commendable devotion to the principles of data protection, the subject would have been in no doubt who the concealed entries related to. In many situations, whether an attempt at concealing the third party's identity will be successful will depend upon a variety of circumstances including the knowledge of the data subject. The example may be postulated of a situation where a neighbour has reported suspicions that a data subject is mistreating a child. If the subject request access, the issue has to be confronted whether deleting the informant's name will suffice to conceal his or her identity. If the subject lives in an isolated area with only one close neighbour any such attempt may be futile. A different conclusion may be reached should the subject live in the centre of a city. A further complicating factor will concern any previous incidents involving the subject and the informant, even whether the subject harbours an unwarranted suspicion that a particular person is responsible for any problems that may befall them.

Beyond the general exception, special provision is made in a number of areas. Once again, records held in connection with the prevention or detection of crime,' the apprehension or prosecution of offenders or the collection or assessment of any tax or duty are exempt from access to the extent that this would prejudice the purpose for which they are held (section 28). The phrase "to the extent that this would prejudice" is significant in every case to which the exception applies. If only elements of the data are covered by an exception, this must be separated and the remainder of the information supplied to the enquiring subject. One major problem may be that no indication need be given to the subject of the fact that an exception has been relied upon. In the extreme case where all of the data was regarded as being covered by the terms of an exception, the reply could lawfully be given to the subject that "We do not hold any relevant personal data of which you are the subject". Such a response may well be misinterpreted by the subject, although it is difficult to imagine how the request might be dealt with in any other way. Informing the subject that data is held but that the access request is being denied subject to the terms of an exception might be as damaging to the purpose of, for example, crime prevention, as would disclosure of the data. Again, it is the absence of procedural safeguards which constitutes the major cause for concern in that no intimation need be made to the Registrar of the fact that an exception has been relied upon. In the event, however, that a subject suspects that data has been withheld, a complaint may be made to the Registrar who may require the user to justify their conduct in the circumstances of the particular case and may, through the service of an enforcement notice, require that data be supplied to the data subject. Such control over the record keeping activities of law enforcement agencies constitutes a significant innovation for the Data Protection Act.

As with the non-disclosure exemptions, a second condition requires that it be demonstrated that the grant of access would prejudice the purpose for which the data is held. In most cases this may be non-problematic although in the situation where the record indicates knowledge that a subject is planning to commit a criminal offence, it might be argued that the interests of crime prevention would best be served by informing the subject of the fact that his or her plans are known to the authorities.

In the case of medical data the right of access is generally to apply, subject to the proviso that access may be denied when in the opinion of a relevant medical professional the grant of access would cause serious harm to the subject's physical or mental health. It is difficult to conceive of any circumstances where this provision might apply in respect of physical health, not least because in this area the subject is almost certain to be aware that records will be kept. Any form of denial will effectively say to the subject, "we will not tell you what is on your record because it will make you seriously ill". It is doubtful whether this will be any more comforting to the patient than to be confronted with the record. The provision may be more relevant in the case of psychiatric illness although the ground for the denial may in many cases lie as much in the fact that the data relates to third parties as to a concern for the subject's health.

Broadly similar restrictions upon the extent of subject access apply where data is held for social work purposes. The provisions here are somewhat looser than those pertaining to health data. In addition to access requests being rejected out of consideration for the subject's physical or mental health, the somewhat nebulous ground of emotional condition is included in the list. Further, whilst decisions to deny access to medical records may only be made by a relevant medical professional - a term which is extensively defined in the enabling regulations - no provision is made as to the qualifications of the person who may determine whether a request for access to social work data is to be accepted or rejected.

Implementation of the proposed European Union Directive would require significant changes to present UK practice in these areas. The proposal recognises the need to make special provision to regulate the manner in which access to medical and social work data is obtained. A practice utilised in a number of other systems is for the data to be revealed to the subject by a medical professional rather than the more common provision of a written transcript. The proposal confers primacy upon the subject's right to seek access and this will override any concerns held by medical professionals as to the potentially adverse effects. A similar provision currently operates in the United Kingdom in respect of access requests which are made by an adoptive child for information relating to his or her natural parents. Here it is a condition of the request being granted that the child first accept counselling as to its potential implications. Following this, the decision whether to proceed is one entirely for the child.

A variety of more specialised exceptions apply to the access provisions. These include the situations where data is held under the protection of legal professional privilege, where it relates to the making of judicial appointments and, and analogous to the provisions relating to criminal investigation and prosecution, to data which is held by certain regulatory bodies such as Lloyds and the Stock Exchange. Further provisions regulate student access to examination records. Here, users may respond within the normal 40 day period and be subject to the general rules. In the case of some major examinations, such as the SCE Ordinary and Higher Grade examinations, the marking process may extend beyond this period. An option is provided to the data user allowing compliance with a request for access to be delayed until 40 days after the publication of the results, subject to a maximum period of six months. Exercise of this option carries a not insignificant penalty in that the subject then has to be supplied not only with information relating to the marks finally awarded but also with any other material, perhaps in the form of provisional marks which were recorded at any time subsequent to receipt of the request for access.

Matters Arising Subsequent to Access

In many situations, obtaining access to data will constitute an end in itself. A variety of options are made available to the data subject in the event that objection is taken to all or part of the data which is revealed. The basis upon which any complaint may be pursued will rest in an allegation that a breach of one or more of the data protection principles has occurred. In the event that a complaint to the data user fails to resolve the issue, the most attractive option for the subject may be to raise the matter with the Data Protection Registrar. The Act provides that the Registrar "may consider any complaint that any of the data protection principles or any provision of this Act have been contravened and shall do so if the complaint appears to him to raise a matter of substance and to have been made without undue delay by a person directly affected" (section 36). Where the Registrar undertakes an enquiry, the data subject is to be informed of its findings. Although the formulation confers a great deal of discretion on the Registrar, much of his efforts have been directed at following up complaints from data subjects.

A number of rights and remedies are conferred directly upon data subjects. In the event that the subject disputes the accuracy of any personal data held, it is provided that the Court may order the rectification of any errors of fact and also of any expressions of opinion which appear to be based on that error (section 24). This appears a rather strange provision. It echoes the issue discussed previously, who statements of opinion and intention might be regarded as belonging to. Although there is a distinction between holding a particular opinion and recording that opinion, the provision does appear capable of threatening a user's freedoms. As an alternative to ordering the amendment of the data, the court may order that it be supplemented by such further statement as may be directed. To date, there do not appear to have been any cases brought under these provisions of the Act and it is uncertain how the available options will be exercised. One scenario illustrates some of the difficult issues which may arise. Increasingly, newspapers and journals maintain copies of past issues in an electronic data base. Any issues of a newspaper will contain a great deal of personal data. The operation of a data base is very likely to involve processing as defined in the Data Protection Act. In the not unprecedented event that a story is wrong, the subject concerned would have the right to seek rectification. The information as held in the data base is presented as the contents of particular issues of the journal in question. Correcting errors might be justifiable from the perspective of the aggrieved subject but it would render the data base unreliable as a historical record. In such a case it may well be that the addition of a notice of correction would be preferable to the amendment of the text to produce a more accurate version.

One limitation upon the subject's right to require the rectification of errors is that it extends only to data held by a particular user. In many cases, the inaccurate data will have been passed on to third parties so that the invidious effects of the error will survive its expulsion from the original user's records. Under the Consumer Credit Act 1974 it is provided that notification of any change made to a record pursuant to the exercise of a subject's right of access is to be given to any third party who had received the information in question within the previous six months (Consumer Credit (Credit Reference Agency) Regulations 1977). Although attempts were made to include similar provisions in the Data Protection Act, these were rejected on the basis that it would put an unfair burden upon data users. The European Union proposals require, however that third parties be notified of any rectification or erasure (Article 13(4)). Once again, it is clear that the new proposals give primacy to the rights of the subject over the operational convenience of the user.

In the event that data is inaccurate, the Act provides that a subject may claim compensation for any damage and distress which the error has caused (section 22). This action will be additional to any claims which may be brought under more traditional headings such as breach of contract or defamation. The use of the formulation "damage and distress" entails that a measure of financial loss will be a prerequisite to any action. This will serve to limit significantly the scope of the action. Although inaccurate data may cause opportunities to be lost, for example where a subject is denied credit facilities following receipt of an inaccurate and unfavourable report by a credit reference agency, these will not be considered compensatable.

Data Protection in Perspective

The current European proposals represent a compromise between the comparatively *laissez faire* approach adopted in the Data Protection Act and the more stringent principle of informational self-determination which constitutes a feature of the German system.

The proper role of a system of data protection remains a subject for debate. The concept of subject access is one which few would criticise, yet it may be queried how far it is of special relevance to automated data processing. The rationale behind the concept is clear. If decisions affecting individuals are to be made on the basis of recorded information, equity requires that they should be able to verify its accuracy. In most of the instances where an individual may wish to see what information is recorded about her the fact of a computer's involvement will be purely incidental. Indeed in a number of the most sensitive areas, such as educational records, health records and credit reference agency files, the right of subject access operates regardless of the format in which the information is held. Subject access under the Data Protection Act may be seen as a specific instantiation of a much wider phenomenon. Particular note may be taken of the proposal contained in the recent White Paper on Open Government (1993, Cmd. 2290) that the individual's right of access should, subject to exceptions, extend to all personal information held by government agencies regardless of the format in which it was held.

One perhaps unfortunate consequence of the individual focus of data protection legislation is that too little attention is paid to the societal implications of data processing. Subject access asserts the primacy of the individual. Much data processing subverts individual personality in a sea of anonymous, aggregate data. By concentrating on abusive conduct, too little attention is paid to the desirability of what is becoming the norm. In a number of cases, subject access appears to have proved more of a prison than a refuge for the data subject. A number of instances have been reported of employers requiring prospective employees to exercise their new-found right of subject access to obtain a copy of their criminal record - or confirmation that no such record exists. It may also be possible to require the provision of exact examination results rather than a pass/fail indication, to require details of medical records. The European Union proposal suggests that individuals should be entitled to refuse a requirement by a third party that access rights should be exercised on their behalf. It appears unlikely that matters may be resolved so simply. At present, an individual is under no obligation to supply the information described above. Short of rendering it illegal for a third party to receive data obtained pursuant to subject access, the imbalance of power that frequently exists in these situations may entail that even the mildest expression of interest on the part of a potential employer will be regarded as akin to a command.

The Act has had some high profile successes. The effect of the enforcement orders served on the four leading credit reference agencies has brought about major changes in their method of operation. In a sense, however, it may be that the victory is pyrrhic. Certainly, a number of data subjects will benefit from wider access to credit because they are no longer tainted by the activities of others who have lived at the same address. It was suggested on behalf of the agencies that if this form of processing were to be prohibited, the effect might be that whole areas might become credit ghettos. The use of credit scoring as a technique for profiling credit applicants may also prove more attractive. The consequence may be that individuals may be denied credit not because of their own record, not because of information held concerning some other individual but because of the processing of aggregate data relating to a large number of individually unidentifiable decisions. This may be even less tolerant of the non-conformist or eccentric individual than is the present system. The European proposals recognise this danger by providing that decisions should not be made purely as a result of automatic processing but that there should be some level of human decision-making.

The Act has created a bureaucracy. Even the term "Registrar" is redolent of form filling and filing. The Committee on Data Protection in their report used the term used the term "Data Protection Authority". In other states the word "Commissioner" is used. It may be that the choice of terminology is indicative of the lack of commitment by the Government at the time of the Act's passage. Although there can be no complaint about the energetic manner in which the Registrar has exercised his role, in too many respects the office operates on the periphery of the key issues. Given the fact that many significant forms of data processing function in the public sector, it may not be unreasonable to see the muzzling of the Registrar as motivated by a concern to avoid independent scrutiny.

Chapter Four

Intellectual Property and the Computer

Introduction

For centuries intellectual (or industrial) property rights have been regarded as a somewhat arcane area of the law. Times are changing. With the increasing importance of the service sector to national economies, attention increasingly requires to be directed to the means of protecting investment in intellectual rather than tangible property. The twin pillars of the intellectual property system are the concepts of patents and copyright. Traditionally, patents have provided the means for protecting and rewarding the practical work of inventors, whilst copyright functions in more aesthetic areas of human activity such as music, art and literature.

The first recorded patent statute was enacted in Venice in 1474. In England, the first statutory intervention occurred with the enactment of the Statute of Monopolies in 1624 which sought to put an end to the Crown's grants of monopolies. For Scotland, patents continued to be issued under the Royal prerogative until the Act of Union had the effect of extending the provisions of the Statute of Monopolies to Scotland. Today, United Kingdom patents are issued under the terms of the Patents Act 1977. An inventor may also apply for a European patent subject to the provisions of the European Patent Convention. The extent to which software-related inventions may be awarded a patent is a matter of some controversy. Both the Act and the Convention state that a patent may not be awarded for a "program for a computer". It has been recognised however, that an invention is not to be barred from patentability because it contains computer programs, and even that a claim will be considered where the novelty resides only in the program-related aspects. Although the topic of software patents has raised considerable passions especially in the United States, the exacting requirements of novelty and inventiveness which constitute a feature of the patent system seem likely to ensure that the role of patents remains on the periphery of the topic. Primacy, at least for the present, rests with the copyright system which will constitute the subject of the remainder of this chapter.

The Copyright System

The law of copyright developed from the eighteenth century with the enactment of the Copyright Act of 1709. As the name suggests, copyright is concerned with the right to make copies of a work. Such a right only assumed practical importance with the development of technology in the form of the printing press which permitted multiple copies to be made of a work. Initially, the new technology was seen by both religious and secular authorities as posing a threat to their own ability to control the dissemination of information and knowledge, and its exploitation was controlled by requiring that a licence be obtained in respect of every publication. Under such a regime, questions concerning the extent of any property rights in works were of very limited significance. A party in receipt of a licence could make copies in accordance with its terms. Persons who did not hold a licence would face sanctions imposed by the licensing authorities were they to venture to print copies.

Government control over publishing was abolished towards the end of the seventeenth century. From this point, the question who would possess the right to produce copies of a work began to assume real economic significance. The same technology which would allow an author (or a publisher) to produce multiple copies of a work for profitable distribution could equally well be used by others to produce competing works. Almost for the first time therefore, the question required to be resolved whether the author of a work (or in practice the publisher to whom any rights would be assigned) possesses a property-related interest in the work sufficient to allow them to prevent or seek a remedy for any unauthorised reproduction. In 1710 the first copyright statute was passed which conferred an exclusive right upon an author or his or her assignee in respect of a work which was registered with the Stationers' Company. The right would subsist for a period of 28 years.

The copyright system has been subject to periodic amendment in the intervening centuries. The requirement to register a work as a pre-requisite for its protection was limited by the Copyright Act of 1842 and abolished by the Copyright Act of 1911 which also extended the duration of protection to a maximum of 50 years after the death of the author[1]. Copyright contains many of the attributes of property; indeed the Copyright, Designs and Patents Act of 1988 states expressly that "(c)opyright is a property right which subsists in the following categories of work ...". Copyright can be bought and sold and any copyrights will form part of an author's estate upon his or her death. Copyright, however, remains a special form of property and the passage of two and a half centuries has done nothing to challenge the validity of Lord Kames observation that "it is a statutory property, and not a property in any just sense to be attended with any of the effects of property at common law" (Kames, *Rem. Dec* Mor. 8298).

As copyright has developed in the United Kingdom, it has come to protect virtually every form of recorded information. Over the years, the scope of copyright has expanded to keep pace with technical developments. Thus the Copyright Act of 1911 brought the products of the fledgling film industry into the categories of protected works. The invention of the phonograph also saw sound recordings becoming a subject for protection whilst the Copyright Act of 1956 extended the scope of protection to include television broadcasts.

These events indicate that copyright has proved a flexible concept, capable of being applied to the output of new forms of technology. In the early days of computerisation, there was little concern for the legal protection of the creative and intellectual efforts which went into the development of computer programs. The principal reason for this was that equipment was supplied as a unit with the same supplier being responsible for both hardware and software components. As software could only be used in conjunction with the hardware for which it was designed, there was little incentive to attempt to make unauthorised copies.

From the 1960s this system began to break down and issues of intellectual property rights began to surface. The first wave of cases concerned the question whether computer programs could be regarded as protected under the law of copyright. Although the matter was never determined by the higher courts, the view was favoured in a number of interlocutory decisions that computer programs should be protected as a species of literary work. Although the relationship between the somewhat impenetrable (at least to the layperson) lines of code which make up any program and a novel or other form of literary work appears somewhat obscure, the fact that items such as football fixture lists and even tide tables and tables of logarithms had been regarded as qualifying for protection lent considerable support to such an approach.

Any question whether computer programs were entitled to copyright protection was resolved with the enactment of the Copyright (Computer Software) (Amendment) Act of 1985. The terms of this measure were restated in the Copyright, Designs and Patents Act which, subject to amendments made in 1992 to incorporate the provisions of the EEC Directive on the Legal Protection of Computer Programs (Council Directive 91/250/EEC. OJ 1991 No L122/42), constitutes the current copyright regime. Subject to the most minor quibbles concerning extremely small computer programs, there is no doubt that the act of copying a program will constitute an infringement of copyright. Computer programs possess an additional dimension which makes their location in the category of literary works somewhat uneasy. Certainly, a program's code can be so regarded but any program will also have an on-screen appearance. This can be replicated even though there may be no similarity at the level of the code. One of the most controversial issues in the intellectual property field concerns the extent to which non-literal copying, replication of what used to be called the "look and feel" of a computer program, will be permitted.

Copyright and Software

Much is written and spoken today on the subject of software piracy - the producing and supplying of computer programs which infringe copyright in an original work. Estimates have put the world-wide losses caused by such activities at some $12.8 billion with almost 40% of this loss being incurred within Europe. In terms of numbers, it has been suggested that 13 unauthorised copies are made of every computer game. For business related software the ratio is calculated at 4 to 1[2]. In Russia it has even been calculated that some 98-99% of copies are unauthorised. As with estimates of the scale of computer crime, these calculations are based on particular sets of definitions and assumptions which may be open to challenge. In particular, if software piracy could be stopped overnight, it seems unlikely that the sales of computer games would rise thirteen-fold. Indeed, it might be argued that, deprived of the possibility of obtaining cheap software, some potential users would determine not to purchase a computer. Elimination of piracy might therefore damage the sales of hardware producers.

In many instances, software piracy will raise no significant legal issues. As stated above, the unadorned act of copying the contents of a computer program will constitute an infringement of copyright. In this situation, a conflict of interests between equipment producers and copyright owners has been a notable feature of recent years. The problem, of course, is not unique to computers. In almost every area of copyright, technological developments are making it easier for copyright infringement to occur. The ubiquitous photocopier makes us all potential copyright infringers to an extent undreamed of twenty years ago. The development of the cassette recorder and in particular its incorporation into musical systems including a record player and radio created a new generation of domestic infringers. With the advent of systems containing two cassette recorders allowing copies to be made of tapes (often in less than the normal playing time of the original), the attempt was made by representatives of copyright owners to seek recourse from those producers who were putting technology which was almost certainly going to be used for unlawful purposes onto the market. In the case of *CBS Songs Ltd v Amstrad Consumer Electronics* [1988] AC 1013 however, the House of Lords rejected all arguments to this effect. Even though the producer's promotion of the equipment was criticised as "deplorable" and "cynical", the fact that it was capable of being put to legitimate uses sufficed to exempt the producer from any form of liability.

In the software field, although it is possible for a software producer to utilise techniques to make copying difficult, the use of these has met with considerable customer resistance, and most of the anti-copying devices can be overcome by a reasonably skilled user. In general, copying a computer program is a very simple task. The contents of a disk can be copied in seconds using standard equipment. In one significant respect, the producers of computer programs are more vulnerable to those who wish to copy their works than most other copyright owners. Where devices such as photocopiers or cassette recorders are used to copy a protected work, the copy will be of inferior quality to the original. If the process is repeated, each generation of copies will show a further reduction in quality, soon reaching the point where it may be unusable for any practical purposes. Because of the digital nature of computer programs every copy of a program will be identical to the original. A fiftieth generation copy will be identical to the original. Much the same applies to the musical contents of compact discs and strenuous efforts were made by copyright bodies to prevent the marketing - or at least require the incorporation of anti-copying devices - of digital tape recorders.

Although it may be stated as a general rule that the reproduction of a protected work constitutes infringement, problems arise in reconciling the claims of copyright owner and legitimate user. Two issues may be cited as illustrative of this topic. First, because of the manner in which a computer functions, on every occasion when a program is used, its contents are copied from a permanent storage location - which may be on a floppy disk or a segment of a computer's hard disk - to a temporary working location. Use of a computer program, therefore, calls for its reproduction, a situation which is not found with more traditional literary works. A second issue concerns the entitlement of a user to make a second copy of a computer program to be brought into use in the event that the original copy is damaged or destroyed. Again, whilst it would be difficult to argue that the purchaser of a book would be entitled to copy its contents against the eventuality that the original were destroyed, computer programs and the devices upon which they are stored are much more fragile creatures. A coffee stain or ink spot will not prevent the book being used for its intended purpose. An electronic equivalent is likely to render both the program and the user's investment worthless.

The 1988 Act remained silent in respect of both of these issues. This created a potentially absurd scenario whereby users would pay considerable sums to acquire a copy of a computer program only to be faced with a claim alleging copyright infringement were they to be bold enough to use it. Although the point was never tested before the courts, it is likely that such a result could have been avoided by the implication of a term into the contract of supply permitting normal use of the program - although the question what might be considered normal use would itself often admit of no easy answer. Implying a term permitting the making of a back-up copy might be more difficult to justify. The practical solution adopted by most suppliers was to issue users with a licence permitting both use of the software and the making of a back-up copy. The downside of such licences was that they would normally also exclude any form of liability on the part of the producer and/or supplier. As a matter of contract law, the enforceability of such licences is open to question. In the vast majority of cases, a contract for the supply of software is concluded before the customer becomes aware of the licence which is normally contained inside the program's packaging. Coupled with the fact that the licence is offered by a producer whilst the program may well have been supplied by a retailer, it must be likely that the terms of the licence will be regarded as constituting a further offer which may be either accepted or rejected by the customer. The difficulty, of course, was that the customer might require the positive aspects of the licence in order lawfully to put the program to its intended and reasonable use. Subject to the possible intervention of the Unfair Contract Terms Act 1977, the price would be the denial of all remedies in the event that the program should prove defective.

To an extent these issues were addressed in the European Directive of 1991. As implemented by the Copyright (Computer Programs) Regulations 1992 (SI

1992 No 3233), it is now provided that although the copyright owner retains the exclusive right to reproduce the work, such copying as occurs in the course of the normal use of the program is not to constitute infringement when it is conducted by a lawful user (regulation 8 inserting a new section 50C into the 1988 Act). Perhaps surprisingly, this right may be excluded by the terms of an agreement. For the first time, therefore, a use right forms part of the United Kingdom copyright regime. Provision is also made in the Regulations allowing a lawful user to make a back-up copy of a program where this is "necessary" for its operation (section 50A). The use of the word "necessary" (which is also found in the Directive) may rob this provision of any real meaning. It is always advisable to take a back-up copy of a program (many producers advise users to copy the program and to use the copy leaving the original as back-up) but it is implicit in the term "back-up" that the second copy is not necessary for the program to function. It is only in the event that the original copy should suffer damage that the back-up will be required.

Whilst conferring an absolute right to make a back-up copy would have the excessive side effect of depriving a producer of the possibility of utilising anti-copying devices, the conferring of a meaningless right must be considered equally objectionable and leaves users in the situation where they may have little alternative to accepting the terms of a licence.

Error Correction

It is received wisdom that every computer program contains errors or "bugs". In accordance with the requirements of the European Union Directive, it is provided that an authorised user may copy or adapt a program "for the purpose of correcting errors in it" (section 50C). This provision might appear to give a user *carte blanche* to copy a program in the quest to discover errors. An alternative, and perhaps preferable view is that the right will extend only in respect of particular errors which have been discovered by the user in the course of running the program in a normal manner. Even on this basis, uncertainties remain as to the extent of the user's rights. Computer programs are not like other literary works. A typing or grammatical error occurring in a book may be corrected without the act having any impact upon the remainder of the work. The relationship between the various elements of a computer program is much more complex. If an error is discovered in the course of running a program, its cause may lie almost anywhere in the program. If the source of a particular error is detected and a correction made, it cannot be certain that the effects of the change will not manifest themselves in an unexpected and undesirable fashion elsewhere in the program. There is indeed a school of thought in software engineering that suggests that when errors are detected, rather than amending the program, operating procedures should be changed to avoid the conditions which it is known cause the specific error to occur.

Reverse Engineering and De-compilation

When software is supplied to a customer, it will be in a form known as object or machine-readable code. If this were to be viewed by a user it would appear as a series, a very long series of zeros and ones. Obtaining sight of these digits will give little indication as to the manner in which the program is structured. Although it is possible for a program to be written in object code, much more programmer-friendly techniques are available and almost universally utilised. A number of what are referred to as "high level" languages exist - examples are BASIC and FORTRAN. These allow programmers to write their instructions in a language which more closely resembles English although the functional nature of computer programs limits the variations in expression which are a hallmark of more traditional literary works.

Most users, of course, will be concerned only with what a program does rather than the manner in which this is accomplished. Some, however, may have different motives. The practice of reverse engineering has a lengthy history in more traditional industries and typically involves the purchase and dismantling of the products of a competitor. In the computer context, reverse engineering may involve study of the operation of a computer program in order to discover its specifications. This is essentially a process of testing and observation and might involve pressing various keys or combinations of keys in order to discover their effects. The technique known as decompilation may be used as part of this process. Normally involving the use of other computer programs to analyse the object code, the technique seeks to reproduce the original source code.

Computer programs can be divided into two broad categories - operating systems and application programs. An operating system (the best known examples are perhaps MSDOS or Microsoft Windows) contains the basic instructions necessary for a computer to operate. A very simple analogy may be made with a railway system. The gauge of the track and the height and width of tunnels and bridges might be regarded as equivalent to an operating system. They set down basic parameters which must be respected by anyone wishing to build a train to operate on the system. If the track gauge is 4ft 8ins, no matter how technologically advanced an engine might be, it will be quite useless if its wheels are set seven feet apart. In the computer field, programs such as word processing and spreadsheet packages constitute the equivalents of railway engines. They work with the operating system to perform specific applications and must respect its particular requirements.

A producer intending to develop an applications package for use on a particular operating system must be aware of its functional requirements. In most instances, the information necessary will be made available by the producer of the operating system whose own commercial interests will be best served by the widest possible availability of applications to run on the system. In the event that the information is not readily available - or that it is suspected that only partial information has been made available - the attempt may be made to reverse engineer the operating system.

A second occasion for the use of reverse engineering occurs at the level of applications packages. Programs such as word processors and spreadsheets store data in a particular format. In the case of basic text, a widely used standard exists, called ASCII (American Standard Code for Information Interchange). The text of most word processed documents is a much more complex creature. Particular fonts, type size and line spacing will be used. Portions of the text may be printed in *italics* or may be **emboldened** or underlined. These matters are not standardised. A producer intent on developing a new word processing program may wish to discover the codes used by rival producers so that conversion facilities may be built into the new product. From a commercial perspective, existing users are more likely to change to a new program if they can still use documents created using their existing program.

The final form of reverse engineering is the most controversial. Here, the object of the reverse engineering is to discover information about the user interface of an applications package which may then be used as the basis for the attempt to produce a substantially similar package. In early court cases on the point in the United States it was often asserted that the intent was to reproduce the "look and feel" of the original package.

Reverse Engineering and the Law

Given that a lawful user cannot be prevented from using a program for its normal purpose, some aspects of reverse engineering must be considered legitimate. A user who operates the program in a normal fashion in order to study its various aspects will not infringe copyright. Subject to strict conditions, a user will also be given the right to attempt to decompile a program's object code when this is done in order to produce a further program which will be interoperable with the copyright owner's. This would apply with respect to the first and second forms of reverse engineering discussed above The right cannot be excluded by contract but will apply only where the information required has not been made "readily available" by the copyright owner. The term "readily available" appears imprecise. It would not seem to require that the information be supplied free of charge. The levying of excessive charges would obviously be incompatible with the provision, but the question will arise what level is to be so considered. In most cases where interchange information is used in, for example, the word processing programs referred to above, it would appear that this is done under the terms of cross-licensing agreements between the parties involved. A second issue raises more technical questions. Producers of operating systems will normally find it in their own commercial interest to make the information available to those who wish to produce applications to run on the system. In some case, the producer of an operating system will also produce applications packages. The best known example is Microsoft. Although sufficient information concerning its operating system is made available to other producers, the systems have a number of what are referred to as "undocumented calls" and it is frequently asserted that these are used by Microsoft's own applications packages. The situation might be compared to producing a road map of the British Isles which omitted all reference to motorways. A motorist who relied totally on the map would certainly be able find a route between Glasgow and London although the journey might take considerably longer than one making use of the motorway network. Returning to the computer context, it may be queried whether the provision of incomplete information will resurrect the decompilation right. Against this, it may be noted that the legislation makes no mention of the quality of the interconnection which is to be enabled. If comparison is made with the patent system, which requires that an inventor disclose details of the manner in which the invention functions, the duty here is to disclose an effective manner of performing the invention and not necessarily the optimum method. Any claim relating to the sufficiency of disclosure above and beyond that necessary to achieve interoperability might more reasonably lie under the heading of competition law.

The provisions described above apply also where the program under investigation is an applications package. Here the usage of the information acquired will be restricted significantly by the statutory prohibition against using the information to produce a program which will infringe copyright in the original. This is not a prohibition against the production of a competing program. The example was cited above of a word processing program which can import or export to or from other word processing programs. Where legal problems arise is in respect of the third form of reverse engineering described above, where the attempt is made to produce a program which appears to a user to be substantially similar to the original. Copyright issues abound here irrespective of the question whether any decompilation has occurred. These will receive detailed consideration in the following section.

The Limits of Copyright Protection: "Look and Feel" and Other Issues

The purpose of copyright is to protect the expressions which are used by an author (or anyone else responsible for the creation of a protected work). The underlying ideas and concepts are not protected. The distinction between unprotected ideas and protected expressions has long been explicitly recognised in the United States. For the United Kingdom, although judicial decisions are replete with *dicta* to the effect that "it is trite law that there is no copyright in ideas", there is no explicit statutory recognition of this situation although the European Directive does provide that "... ideas and principles which underlie any element of a computer program ... are not protected under this Directive" (article 1(2)). The only reference to this provision in the implementing regulations is a provision voiding any contractual attempt to exclude an authorised user's right to "study or test the functioning of the program in order to understand the ideas and principles which underlie any element" (section 296A(1)(c)).

Although it may be "trite law" that ideas are not protected under the law of copyright, the task of distinguishing between ideas and the manner in which they are expressed is often a difficult one. Indeed, few works will be based upon a single idea. Rather, there will be a number of ideas ranging from the extremely general to the extremely specific at which point they may become inextricably linked with the forms of expression used. Thus the idea may occur to a person for writing a book. Certainly, this aspect of the work cannot be protected under the law of copyright. The thought process may move on to the notion that the work is to be a legal tome and that it is to be concerned with the legal response to aspects of computer-related behaviour. Here it seems certain that we are still in the realm of unprotected ideas. The next idea may concern the main categories of material to be included and the order in which it is to be presented. The creative process may move on with ideas being expressed as to the format of particular sentences and phrases until a complete text is produced, the reproduction of which will constitute a breach of copyright. On this analysis, every expression represents ideas and ideas are nothing until they are expressed. The task for a court is to determine where along the creative spectrum the protection afforded by the law of copyright should begin.

In one of the few United Kingdom cases where copyright has been refused to a written work, the Court of Appeal held in the case of *Exxon Corp v Exxon Insurance Consultants Ltd* [1982] Ch 119 that the single invented word Exxon[3], could not be regarded as a literary work and that another party making use of it was not guilty of infringement of copyright. Beyond this, it is generally recognised that character names and details of the plot of a literary work may obtain copyright protection. Much publicity was recently given to the publication of a sequel to the novel "Gone With the Wind". It is suggested that one of the reasons for the appearance of the work was that the period of copyright protection in the original novel was about to expire. At that time anyone could write such a sequel making use of the character names and any other elements of the original storyline[4]. By commissioning the sequel, the estate of the original author would be able to create what was effectively a new copyright.

Although character names and storylines may be regarded as the subject of copyright, the case of *Green v Broadcasting Corp of New Zealand* [1988] 2 NZLR 490 shows that this approach has its limits. The case concerned a television programme devised by the appellant called "Opportunity Knocks". The programme was effectively a talent contest offering new performers an opportunity to appear on television. The programme was presented by the appellant. Each show followed a particular format with acts being introduced by sponsors, the appellant who presented the show using particular catch phrases. The comparative popularity of the acts with the studio audience was measured using a device referred to as the "Clapometer", whilst a postal ballot was conducted to determine the preferences of the viewing audience. The show ran for a number of years in the United Kingdom. Some time later the appellant discovered that a show of the same name was being produced and broadcast in New Zealand utilising much the same format as the original. An action alleging breach of copyright was raised only to be dismissed by the New Zealand courts, a decision upheld on appeal to the Privy Council. In part the decision was based upon evidential failings on the part of the appellant who was unable to present any detailed scripts pertaining to the programme. Such evidence as was submitted referred to the general format of the show. As Somers J commented in the New Zealand Court of Appeals:

> The scripts, as I understand them, could not constitute a dramatic work. They could not themselves be acted or performed which I take to be the essence of such a work for they were no more than a general scheme for a proposed entertainment (p 497).

Dismissing the appeal, the judge concluded:

> Not surprisingly he (Mr Green) feels his ideas have been appropriated. But that, I am afraid, is all that has happened. Whether taken item by item or as a whole I am of opinion that the scripts as they are inferred to be from the description given in evidence did not themselves do more than express a general idea or concept for a talent quest and hence were not the subject matter of copyright (p 498).

Concurring, Casey J made reference to an article by an American commentator which suggested that:

> Formats are thus an unusual sort of literary creation. Unlike books, they are not meant for reading. Unlike plays, they are not capable of being performed. Unlike synopses, their use entails more than the expansion of a story outline into a script. Their unique function is to provide the unifying element which makes a series attractive - if not addictive - to its viewers.

Again reference was made to the sense of grievance which might by felt by a person in Mr Green's position who considered that there had been "piracy of a good entertainment idea" (p 504). "Nevertheless", he concluded:

> the overall interests of society in maintaining the free exchange and ability to develop ideas must also be considered. Any extension of the defined breadth of copyright protection must be approached with caution and is probably best left to the informed decision of the legislature (p 504).

It is a moot point whether the presence of a detailed script making reference to the catch phrases and features of the show might have prompted a different conclusion. In the case of *Harman Pictures v Osborne* [1967] 2 All ER 324 an interlocutory injunction was sought to prevent the making of a film on the Charge of the Light Brigade whose script was alleged to infringe copyright in a book written on the subject. Given the nature of the proceedings, the precedential value of the decision is limited but the absence of any attempt by the defendant to identify sufficient alternative sources for their work to rebut the evidence of similarity was held sufficient to justify the grant of an injunction.

A relevant aspect of this case for the present work is that the nature of both the book and the film was constrained to some extent by external factors. The Charge of the Light Brigade was a historic reality. Reference would be expected in any work on the topic to the key characters involved and to the major events. This situation may occur in many other contexts. The information in a telephone or trade directory is factual information and, at least in respect of alphabetical listings, virtually no discretion is afforded to a person seeking to compile such a work. In the United States, the Supreme Court has held in the case of *Feist v Rural Telephone Inc* 111 Sup Ct Rep 1282 (1991) that the functional constraints identified above were such that no copyright subsisted in a telephone directory as there was insufficient originality involved in its compilation. It may be doubted whether the same decision would be reached in proceedings before a United Kingdom court. Here, the requirement that a work be original has been interpreted as requiring nothing more than that it is not copied from an original source. Indeed, in the case of *Waterlow Directories Ltd v Reed Information Services Ltd (The Times*, 11 October 1990) copyright was held to subsist in alphabetic listings of English solicitors arranged by town.

Incidents such as that at issue in *Harman Pictures* indicate that the exact reproduction of a protected work is not necessary in order to establish infringement. The Copyright Designs and Patents Act, restating the provisions of earlier statutes, states specifically that the making of an adaptation of a protected work, in circumstances where there may be few if any signs of literal similarities between the two works, will constitute infringement. The basic infringing act is referred to as that of reproducing the protected work or a substantial part thereof. The concept of reproduction is broader than that of copying. By moving away from the situation where copying of a work was the sole criteria for infringement, the basis of the system rests more in the element of unfair exploitation of the work of another. One of the most frequently quoted dicta in the area is that of Petersen J in the case of *University of London Press Ltd v University Tutorial Press Ltd* [1916] 2 Ch 601 to the effect that "what is worth copying is worth protecting". Copyright infringement will typically be established by showing that a defendant enjoyed access to a protected work and subsequently produced a work which indicated that he had unfairly exploited the work. In *Harman Pictures*, the allegation was that the screenplay was based excessively upon one work of reference. An even more extreme case is that of *Elanco Products v Mandops* [1980] RPC 213. Here the plaintiff company held a patent in a herbicide. In marketing the product, it supplied detailed instructions for use, these being based on its research and experiences of the product and intended to ensure its maximum effectiveness. When the patent expired it was, of course, open to anyone else to produce the herbicide and this was done by the defendant. In addition to reproducing the plaintiff's product, it also reproduced their instructions. This prompted an objection from the plaintiff and resulted in the defendant making two attempts to modify the terms of the instructions. The changes made failed to satisfy the plaintiff who instituted proceedings alleging that the defendant's instructions infringed their copyright and seeking an interlocutory injunction to prevent the continued use of the instructions pending a trial.

By the time the copyright action was instituted, the defendant's instructions bore few similarities to those originally produced by the plaintiff. Nonetheless, it was held that the copyright had been infringed, Goff L J ruling that:

> It may well be that if the respondents had in fact at the start simply looked at the available information ... and from that decided what they would put in their literature and how they would express it, the appellants would at least have had considerable difficulty in bringing home any charge of infringement, even having regard to the evidence, if the results had been exceedingly similar and the selection of items had been the same. But they chose, on the evidence as it stands at the moment, to proceed by making a simple ... copy, and then they proceeded to revise it. It may well be that the result produced in that way is an infringement.

Given that a patent specification serves as a set of instructions concerning the manner in which the invention is to be performed, the decision in *Elanco* might be criticised as marking an unwarranted extension to the duration of protection offered to a patent holder. Whilst it must be conceded that the detailed instructions for the application of the herbicide would not be contained in the patent specification, the fact that the plaintiff had enjoyed what might have been a twenty-year monopoly over the commercial exploitation of the product must have limited significantly the scope and the incentive for others to conduct research in the field. On a more literary analysis, of course, it is clear that the defendant's conduct, even with respect to the third draft of the instructions, could be regarded as a form of plagiarism. A difficulty with the decision in *Elanco* and, as we shall see, with cases involving copyright in computer programs, may come from the attempt to apply literary criteria to functional and practical works. Significant differences do exist between the two categories of work. In particular, whilst diversity of expression is desirable in a literary context, it may have the opposite effect in the realm of product instructions. Where users have become accustomed to particular instructions for a product as potentially dangerous as a herbicide, there may be undesirable possibilities for confusion and error if the product is supplied with apparently different instructions.

Although a number of English cases considered the extent of copyright protection in software at the interlocutory level, it was only in 1993 with the case of *John Richardson Computers Ltd v Flanders and Chemtec Ltd* [1994] FSR 144, that the issues were considered in a full hearing. At issue in this case was a computer program designed for use by pharmacists. The program, which was developed to run on the then popular BBC micro-computers, performed a number of tasks. Principally, when the computer was attached to a printer to would automate and simplify the task of preparing dosage instructions to be supplied with medicines. The program's other major function was to assist in stock-keeping by keeping a record of the drugs dispensed. The program was marketed by the plaintiff who had also performed a significant amount of work on the original program. Subsequently, the first defendant was employed to work on the project. It was accepted that all relevant copyrights in the work belonged to the plaintiff.

The program achieved considerable commercial success. Relationships between the plaintiff and the defendant were not so fortunate. The defendant resigned from his position although he continued to perform some work for the plaintiff as an independent contractor for a further period of time.

With the advent of the IBM personal computer, one of the plaintiff's major customers expressed interest in a version of the program capable of running on this machine and which could be sold on the Irish market. Following discussions the plaintiff determined not to proceed with the project but at his suggestion the defendant was approached and agreed to perform the work. The program was completed and was sold in Ireland under the name "Pharm-Assist". The defendant subsequently contacted the plaintiff offering him the rights to market the product in the United Kingdom. These discussions proved fruitless and the defendant proceeded to market a modified version of the Pharm-Assist program. At that stage the plaintiff initiated proceedings alleging that "Pharm-Assist" infringed copyright in his original program.

Because of the fact that the programs had been developed to run on different computers, examination of the code used would have revealed few evidences of similarities. The programs did perform the same functions and had very similar appearances when operating on their respective hardware.

In the absence of any relevant UK precedent, the court placed considerable reliance upon the United States case of *Computer Associates v Altai* 982 F 2d 693 (1992). Here, an employee switched employment between the firms, commencing work for the defendants. Unknown to his new employers who put him to work on a project, he had worked on a similar project for his previous employer and had taken a copy of the relevant source code when he left their employ. He completed the task in 4 months only for it to be discovered subsequently that about 30% of the code of the second program was a direct copy from the original. The defendants accepted that this constituted a breach of copyright.

Following discovery of its employee's conduct, the defendant sought to produce a legitimate program which performed the same functions. To achieve this a new team of programmers was put together, selected because none of them had any previous experience on the project. The programmers were given a description of the facilities which were to be developed and were required to produce the programs necessary. The project took some six months to complete and the revised product was put on the market. In circumstances not dissimilar to those at issue in the *Elanco* case discussed above, these subsequent attempts to vitiate an original act of copying did not satisfy the plaintiffs who alleged that the revised version also infringed the copyright in the non-literal aspects of their program.

This argument was rejected by the District Court, a conclusion upheld by the Court of Appeals for the Second Circuit. Although it was recognised that copyright protection had to extend beyond the strictly textual form in order to avoid the situation where a plagiarist could avoid liability by making immaterial variations, it was held that the question whether infringement had occurred could be answered only after making a detailed analysis of the circumstances at issue. In particular, the court recommended the utilisation of a three-stage test - referred to as the "abstraction-filtration-comparison test" in order both to identify the elements of a work which were entitled to protection and to determine whether infringement had occurred.

The first stage of the test involves the court in its own form of reverse engineering. Beginning with the complete program and its code, the process should work back to the basic idea producing what might be considered a chart of the development process.

After the identification of the elements of the original program that are to form the basis of the decision, the filtration stage seeks to determine why particular elements are found in the original program and to filter out or discard those whose presence is due to circumstances which would serve to deny copyright protection. As identified by the courts in *Computer Associates*, these might include aspects of the program whose form is dictated by reason of efficiency. In many cases, there may be a limited number of ways in which a task may be performed effectively. Also identified as factors which might be filtered out were elements of the program whose form was dictated by external factors. Particular reference was made to:

> (1) the mechanical specifications of the computer on which a particular program is intended to run; (2) compatibility requirements of other programs with which a program is intended to run in conjunction; (3) computer manufacturers design standards; (4) demands of the industry being serviced; and (5) widely accepted programming practices within the computer industry.

It is the filtration stage of the *Computer Associates* test which fits least easily into the United Kingdom system. In the United States, the merger doctrine has served to deny copyright protection where an idea can be expressed in a very limited number of ways. Such a doctrine has never formed a feature of the United Kingdom system where the only question to be determined by a court has been whether copying has occurred.

The final stage of the process entails the comparison of the remaining elements of the original program, what was referred to as the "golden nugget" of protected material, against the features of the allegedly infringing program with a view to determining whether any similarities should be regarded as involving a substantial part of the original work and as having been produced as a result of copying rather than by independent creative activities.

The result of the application of this test in *Computer Associates* was a finding that no infringement had occurred. In *Richardson*, Ferris J sought to apply a modified and less technical version in which, after determining the eligibility of the program as a whole for copyright protection - a fairly straightforward matter - the court proceeded to answer the question "whether any similarity attributable to copying which is to be found in the defendants program amounts to the copying of a substantial part of the plaintiff's program?"

The first stage in this process involved an examination of the functions performed by the two programs and the manner in which these were carried out. This revealed seventeen points of similarity concerning the functions performed by the two programs and the manner in which these took place. When these were subjected to more detailed examination, however, six of the points of similarity were considered explicable by reasons other than copying. To give perhaps the simplest illustration, both programs used the same format of date with numbers for day, month and year. Other similarities related to the manner in which the quantity to be prescribed was dealt with before the drug itself was identified. Beyond the fact that only two alternatives were available, evidence was presented indicating substantial commercial demand for the adoption of the quantity first option.

In respect of a further eight similarities, the view was taken either that no copying had occurred or that the similarities did not constitute a substantial part of the original program. An example of the latter situation concerned the inclusion of a feature in both programs whereby the message "operation successful" appeared on the computer monitor accompanied by a double beep. Such a feature was considered lacking in "originality and cannot have required any significant skill or effort to devise it".

In the case of only three of the similarities was the conclusion reached that copying had occurred of a substantial part of the original program. One of these related to the procedures whereby a user could amend entries so as to correct any errors which had been made. Although the need for such a facility would exist in any program, the original routines were unusual in their nature with features that could be regarded as inefficient and misleading to the user. The fact that the later program functioned in the same manner was considered indicative of the fact that it had been copied from the original. It appears to be a feature of cases in this area that similarities of mistakes rather than of valuable features is more damaging to an alleged copyist. Overall, however, such copying as was established in this case was described as constituting "a fairly minor infringement in a few limited respects."

Allegations of copyright were again before the High Court in the case of *Ibcos Computers v Barclays Mercantile Highland Finance and Another* [1994] FSR 275. Again there was a background of the major defendant having worked for the plaintiff on the development of a software product intended for use by agricultural dealers which was marketed under the name ADS. On leaving its employment, he developed a further and competing product which was marketed under the name of Unicorn. The plaintiff alleged that sufficient features of this were copied from the original to constitute an infringement of copyright.

In determining the criteria which would be applied in determining the question whether infringement had occurred, Jacobs J was somewhat critical of the extensive references to the United States decision in *Computer Associates* and warned against "overcitation of US authority based on a statute different from ours". The approach to be adopted was for the court to determine whether there was a sufficient degree of similarity between the two works which, coupled with evidence of access to the original work, would establish an inference of copying. The onus would then switch to the defendant to establish that the similarities were explicable by causes other than copying. Evidence that "functional necessity" served to narrow the range of options open to the defendant would be relevant. Trivial items may well provide the most eloquent testimony. As was said in *Bilhofer v Dixon* [1990] FSR 105:

> It is the resemblances in inessentials, the small, redundant, even mistaken elements of the copyright work which carry the greatest weight. This is because they are the least likely to have been the result of independent design.

In the present case, evidence was presented that the same words were mis-spelled in the same manner, the same headings were used in the two programs and both shared the same bit of code which served no useful purpose for the functioning of the program. Beyond this, there were considerable similarities at the level of the code itself. In respect of one element of the programs it was held that:

> ... there are 22 identical variables, 8 identical labels, 1 identical remark, 31 identical code lines and one identical redundant variable. This to my mind plainly indicates copying and enough in itself to constitute a significant part.

The court recognised in *Ibcos* that copyright protection must extend beyond the literal aspects of the program code to aspects of "program structure" and "design features". In the case of the former element, it was held that copyright subsisted in the compilation of individual programs which made up the ADS system. Although some differences existed between ADS and Unicorn it was held that the defendant had taken "as his starting point the ADS set and that set remains substantially in Unicorn." Although the two programs had a different visual appearance and it was recognised that "Unicorn is undoubtedly to the user a much friendlier program than ADS was at the time", the defendant, it was held had taken "shortcuts by starting with ADS and making considerable additions and modifications."

Conclusions

Comparison of the decisions in *Richardson* and *Ibcos* causes perhaps more confusion than enlightenment. In its essentials, *Ibcos* may be considered a relatively straightforward case of copyright infringement although a number of the surrounding circumstances raise more difficult issues. The fact that the two programs used the same operating system and were designed to run on the same types of computers facilitated both direct copying and its detection. In *Richardson*, the move from the BBC to the IBM system meant that there was far less opportunity for, and evidence of, direct copying. Whilst each case has to be determined on its own merits, the finding of "fairly minor" copyright infringement in *Richardson* is to be contrasted with much more extensive findings in *Ibcos*.

It has always been a feature of copyright that protection has extended beyond the purely literal aspects of a work. Any other approach would allow a party to make the most minor changes in order to escape liability. Without exception, the cases which have been dealt with before the United Kingdom courts, whether at interlocutory level or at the stage of a trial, have been grounded in the situation where there has been a prior relationship between the parties. In most cases this has involved a contract of employment. In these situations there has been access to the most detailed elements of the original program. Ordinary users will obtain a much less detailed picture of the program. It may be possible for such a party to decompile elements of the object code so as obtain access to the source code. Where the goal is to produce a competing rather than an inter-operable product, such an approach may be unnecessary. Where the desire is to replicate elements of the visual appearance of the original program, the necessary information can be acquired merely to studying the program in operation. The writing of the enabling code will then be a comparatively simple matter. In *Computer Associates*, it took only two months longer for the second, clean, version of the software to be produced than was occupied in the making of the original infringing version.

The most intractable problem in applying principles of literal copyright to computer programs is that these possess both passive and active aspects. Even where the same computer language is used there will be a very great number of ways in which even the simplest function may be implemented. To give a mathematical analogy, whilst 2+3=5, so does 1+4 or 8-3. The range of permutations is almost infinite. Protecting software as a literary work is akin to protecting a particular formulation of a question when it is the answer which is all-important.

Two further factors may also be identified as complicating matters yet further. First, the operation of the copyright system may be criticised as paying inadequate regard to the interests of computer users. The acquirer of a computer program will require to invest time and effort in learning how to make use of it. If a change is made to another program, the learning process will have to be commenced anew unless the features of the two programs are similar. Whilst the interests of the readers of literary works are best served by the availability of the most diverse forms of expression possible, different considerations apply with functional objects such as software. The conse-quence of strong copyright protection for computer programs may be to tie a customer into a relationship with the original producer. In the case of *British Leyland Motor Corp Ltd v Armstong Patents Co Ltd* [1986] 1 AllER 850, the House of Lords held that the plaintiffs were not to be permitted to use their copyright in engineering drawings in order to maintain a monopoly in respect of spare parts for their vehicles. The right of car owners to maintain their vehicles was to take precedence over the producer's intellectual property rights. Although the situations are   not precisely comparable in that the purchaser of a computer program is likely to be seeking its replacement rather than its repair, some regard should be paid to the user's interests.

The second factor concerns the implications of intellectual property rights in an employment relationship. Where individuals are employed as software programmers as was the case in *Richardson* and *Ibcos*, it may be extremely difficult to distinguish between their own expertise and the proprietary infor-mation belonging to the employer. Most programmers when faced with a particular task will not attempt to create new code. Rather they will seek to reuse existing modules. These may be taken either from their own portfolio of work and experience or from reference manuals. Too extensive an application of intellectual property rights may inhibit significantly the future career pros-pects of employees.

As was stated at the outset of this chapter, copyright has proved a flexible legal tool. Even the most flexible structures have limits beyond which they cannot be stretched without both causing and suffering damage and it may be that these limits have been reached. In *Computer Associates*, the Court of Appeals commented that:

> Generally, we think that copyright registration - with its indiscriminating availability - is not ideally suited to deal with the highly dynamic technology of computer science. Thus far, many of the decisions in the area reflect the court's attempt to fit the proverbial square peg in a round hole.

and went on to suggest that the patent system might provide a more appropriate regime with protection being dependent upon "exacting up-front novelty and non-obviousness requirements". Considerable concern has however been expressed at the ability of patent examiners to make informed decisions as to novelty and obviousness in the face of such a rapidly changing subject as computer science. It may be that the application of copyright should be restricted to the situation where there is direct copying of a program. This may well encompass most instances of software piracy and many aspects of the decision in *Ibcos*. For the case where a similar product involves independent effort the need may be for a *sui generis* system, perhaps involving compulsory licences, to ensure that the original creator receives a fair reward for the skill and labour expended whilst allowing users to find other sources of supply.

A final reference may be made to the suitability of the legal system for resolving disputes concerned with intellectual property issues in software. In many instances the litigation is prolonged. The trial in *Computer Associates* lasted for eight days, whilst the hearings in the English cases of *Richardson* and *Ibcos* occupied twenty four and thirteen days respectively. The expenses incurred in such lengthy proceedings must inhibit parties taking disputes to the courts whilst a lack of case law furthers a perception of uncertainty as to the legal position. Even in the cases discussed above, the time necessitated to bring the dispute before the courts entails that the decision relates to technology which may be functionally obsolete. The original program in *Richardson* was written for the BBC micro-computer in the early 1980s. This computer had a maximum memory of 96 kilobytes of data. This text has been written on a fairly basic computer of the 1990s which has a memory of 12 megabytes. The new machine is about 125 times more powerful than the old one. Similarly, in *Ibcos* the initial version of the programs at issue was written in 1979. Although court decisions may allocate financial responsibility for past events, it seems unlikely that they can have significant impact upon present and future activities.

Chapter Five

Liability Issues

Introduction

As the preceding discussions have indicated, computers are used increasingly in situations where any malfunction may result in financial or physical loss, damage or injury. The terms "mission" and "safety critical" are often used. In such circumstances, a lawyer's fancy lightly turns to thoughts of liability. Given the range of computer applications and the myriad forms of liability, any work of this nature can present no more than an overview of the issues. Unlike the topics discussed previously, no specific statutory provisions can be identified and case law is extremely limited. This dictates that the approach adopted in this chapter will differ from that of its predecessors. Its aim is, taking account of the major forms of liability, to instantiate situations where loss may result from the operation of computer systems and consider the factors which may influence the allocation and extent of liability.

Prior to considering these issues it is helpful to give brief consideration to the nature of computer software and to the differences which exist between software and the tangible products with which society and the law are more familiar. The first difference of substance may be identified at the level of testing. With a product such as a motor car, it is possible to test every component so as to provide definitive information about its properties. Often, however, testing entails destruction of the item involved and even where this is not the case, it will seldom be commercially feasible to test every specimen of the product. In production, it is possible that some components will be of inferior quality to those tested. A further point is that many, probably most, instances of defects occur as a result of errors at the production stage. Only a portion of products will possess any particular defect and these may not be the ones which are selected for inspection. The conclusion from this analysis is that it is possible to test one item exhaustively but that the results have limited applicability regarding other items of the same type.

The situation is radically different where software is concerned. It is impossible to test even the simplest program in an exhaustive fashion. This is because of the myriad possibilities for interaction (whether desired or not) between the various elements of the program. In the world of popular science much publicity has been given in recent years to what is known as chaos theory. This suggests that every event influences every other event; that the beating of a butterfly's wings has an impact upon the development of a hurricane. On such an analysis, totally accurate weather forecasting will never be practicable because of the impossibility of taking account of all the variables affecting the climate. The theory's hypothesis is reality in a software context. Although software can and should be tested, it has to be accepted that every piece of software will contain errors which may not materialise until a particular and perhaps unrepeatable set of circumstances occurs. Especially where software is used in safety critical functions it is sometimes advocated that where an error is discovered it is preferable to devise procedures to prevent the circumstances recurring than to attempt to modify the software. The argument is that any change to the software may have unanticipated consequences resulting in another error manifesting itself at some time in the future. The cause of a massive failure which paralysed sections of the United States' telecommunications system in 1991 was ultimately traced to changes which had been made in the call routing software[1]. The software contained several million lines of code. Three apparently insignificant lines were changed and chaos ensued. By way of contrast, the operators of London's Docklands Light Railway, whose trains are driven under computer control, took the decision that they would not make any changes to the software after it had passed its acceptance tests. The result was that for several years trains stopped on an a open stretch of line, paused for a few seconds and then continued with their journey. It had been intended to build a station at the site. After the software was accepted the plans were abandoned but the trains remained ignorant of this fact.

The plus side of software testing and production is that although the testing has limitations the nature of the copying is such as to give a very high degree of assurance that every copy which is made will be identical. Production defects are virtually unknown so that test results will be valid for every copy of the software.

Forms of Liability

The nature of legal rights and obligations is dependent in large measure upon the relationship between the parties. The distinction may be of limited significance where the operation of a computer system has resulted in some form of physical damage or injury but will be far more significant when loss is economic in nature. Here it may only be a contracting party who has a right to compensation.

The question whether information could or should be regarded as a form of property has been discussed extensively in previous chapters. A similar debate rages concerning the question whether computer software should be regarded as a product or be dealt with under the law relating to the supply of services. An illustration of this concerns the system of product liability introduced on an EC basis by the Council Directive 85/374 on the approximation of the laws, regulations and administrative provisions of the Member States concerning liability for defective products[2] and implemented in the United

Kingdom under the terms of the Consumer Protection Act 1987. In answer to a question in the European Parliament concerning the scope of the Directive, the Commission stated that:

> the term product is defined as all moveables, with the exception of primary agricultural products ... Consequently, the Directive applies to software

By way of contrast, in a Consultative Note published by the Department of Trade and Industry prior to the enactment of the Act, it was suggested that:

> Special problems arise with those industries dealing with products concerned with information such as books ... and computer software....

and the argument advanced that the legislation should not apply within these sectors. As discussed in relation to copyright, the linkage between books and software is a somewhat strained one, whilst it also appears that the Consultative Note conflates two distinct issues. A book is made up of pieces of paper bound together in some manner and a computer program will normally be supplied on a plastic disk. Paper and plastic must certainly be classed as products. If a book or disk has a sliver of metal embedded in its cover which cuts the hand of a user the item has to be regarded as a defective product. The second and more uncertain issue relates to the informational content of the products. The prevailing view has been as expressed by Denning LJ in the case of *Candler v Crane Christmas* [1951] 2 KB 164 that:

> a scientist or expert ... is not liable to his readers for careless statements in his published works. He publishes his work simply for the purpose of giving information, and not with any particular transaction in mind at all.

In most cases human beings must be credited with the capacity for independent thought and judgement. Their actions will be based on a wider range of inputs than are normally contained in a single publication. The Commission, it is argued, are correct in considering software to be a product. This leads, however, to further issues when software can be considered defective and whether any particular defect can be regarded as having caused injury or damage as defined in the legislation.

In considering the application of the product liability regime three situations might be identified. The first is where the software controls directly some object or function and where any failure might result in injury or damage. Next we have situations where a software failure may set up a dangerous situation but where the existence of a causal link between defect and damage may be unclear. Finally, consideration will be given to the situation where a computer system gives information or advice to a human user who acts on this only for injury or damage to result.

Computers Can Damage Your Health

In 1829 the directors of the embryonic Liverpool and Manchester railway determined to hold a contest to find the most suitable form of motive power and devised a set of elaborate performance specifications. Items such as size weight, haulage power and speed were dealt with. There was even provision, ignored in practice, that locomotives should consume their own smoke. The specification, however, made no mention of brakes, an omission which was to have tragic consequences when Lord Huskisson stepped onto the track in front of an oncoming train.

Failure to consider the means of stopping a locomotive might appear exceptionally culpable. Prior to the invention of the steam engine, however, the major problem with transport had been to move objects. Stopping them had been a matter of little concern. From this standpoint, the omission of specifications regarding braking capabilities might be viewed rather more charitably. Many of the problems with software can be traced to deficiencies in the original specification. One of the best known concepts in science fiction is Isaac Asimov's laws of robotics. The laws state that:

1.   A robot may not injure a human being, or, through inaction, allow a human being to come to harm.
2   A robot must obey the orders given to it by human beings, except where such orders would conflict with the First Law.
3   A robot must protect its own existence as long as such protection does not conflict with the First or Second Laws.

The laws of robotics might be seen as equivalent to the human ten commandments. As we all know, the complexities of life are such that the commandments provide only the most general guidance and constantly require to be interpreted and defined in the light of events. In the real world, unfortunately, incidents have occurred of humans being killed by robots. In one case reported in the computer press, a factory worker was killed when he strayed into an area where a robot was operating and was pinned between the robot and a steel pole. The cause of the accident was that the robot had been programmed to complete its work without stopping. Notices had been displayed warning employees against entering the robot's area of operation but the question might arise, not least under the requirements of the Health and Safety at Work legislation, whether this was sufficient to ensure a safe system of work.

In other situations, computer programs may perform similar functions in a more opaque fashion. An example might be where computers control the flight of an airplane. An automatic pilot is essentially a form of robot. At a more down-to-earth level, many motor cars rely upon computers to control the operation of items such as anti-lock braking systems. In both examples, the potentially fatal consequences of a failure on the part of the computer system are all too obvious. In one recent air crash, it has been speculated that a dispute between the human and the automatic pilots may have been responsible for the accident and it is a frequent complaint that those responsible for designing (specifying) computer systems take inadequate account of human frailties and our propensity to push the wrong button or stray from normal procedures.

Since the enactment of the Consumer Protection Act the producer of a defective product has been held strictly liable for any personal injury resulting from its operation. Liability is also imposed in respect of any damage to private (non-commercial) property. As will be discussed below, there is uncertainty whether a computer program might be regarded as a product for the purposes of either the Consumer Protection or the Sale of Goods Acts. This is a matter of little significance in the situation described above where the program controls directly the operation of a physical object which in turn causes death or personal injury. What is of more significance is the determination when the product is to be considered defective and, given that liability under the Consumer Protection Act is strict rather than absolute, whether any defences might be available.

Under the terms of the Consumer Protection Act a product is to be considered defective when it fails to provide the level of safety that "persons generally are entitled to expect". In most cases this must mean that a party will not come to any harm as a result of coming into contact with the product. Account must be taken of the manner in which the product is used. If a user cuts a finger whilst wielding a knife, it would generally be recognised that the fault lay with the user rather than the product. In similar fashion, although air passengers might reasonably expect that they will be carried safely to their destination, the producer of an airplane would not be held responsible for an accident caused by pilot error.

In real life it may seldom be the case that a single factor is responsible for an accident. The Consumer Protection Act is concerned only with the liability which may be incurred by the producer (or in some cases the supplier or importer of a product). In many instances, other forms of liability may also arise. In the example of the robot, it is likely that the worker would have been in a contractual relationship with the factory owner who might be liable for breach of the statutory duty to provide a safe system of work. In the airplane example, passengers would have had a contract of carriage (itself subject to the terms of international Conventions) with the airline involved.

It is also the case that risks may be inherent to an activity. The Act provides that a product is not to be considered defective solely because "the safety of a product which is supplied after that time is greater than the safety of the product in question". The example might be put forward of two cars travelling side by side along a road, each travelling at 80 kph. Without warning, a hole appears in the road 30 metres ahead. Seconds later, one car has stopped short of the obstacle whilst the other has disappeared into the bowels of the earth. Discounting factors such as driver reaction, this might appear indicative that the second car is defective. Further investigations reveal that the first car was produced in 1994 and the second in 1954. If it is further discovered that the average stopping distance for a 1954 built car travelling at 80 kph was 35 metres, this conclusion might have to be revised. Products have to be assessed against their contemporaries rather than their successors, although a distinction must be drawn between the situation described above where a certain level of performance represents the state of the art and that where a failure might be in accordance with expectations. The concept of perfection is seldom a realistic goal and it may be anticipated, for example, that an airplane engine will fail once in ten thousand hours of flight. It might be further calculated that the risks of both engines failing on a twin engined plane would be once for every 100 million hours of flight. In the event such a dual failure occurred and injury resulted, it would be no defence for the producer to establish that the failure rate was in line with the calculations and that the state of the technical art did not permit them to build a more robust product. These issues will be considered more fully in the context of the development risks defence.

As computer applications become more sophisticated, the risk analysis referred to above may become a matter of increasing complexity. It has been suggested that the technology is such that robot surgeons could perform operations to narrower tolerances than any human could attain. This is perceived as having particular advantages in surgery for the removal of brain tumours. By being able to cut more precisely, a robot could remove a greater proportion of the tumour, thereby improving the patient's prognosis. Any operation can go wrong. In the event that a surgical procedure goes wrong, a patient seeking compensation has presently to establish negligence on the part of the surgeon. If the surgeon is a robot it may be that the provisions of the Consumer Protection Act will impose strict liability. The robot will thus be judged more harshly than the human. Other ethical and legal considerations aside, such a possibility may well deter hospital authorities from utilising the new technology. It may be that the law and lawyers are better equipped to assess the nebulous nature of human conduct than the statistical precision which characterises computer applications.

Problems of Causation

During 1992 considerable publicity was given to failures in a computer system supplied to and operated by the London Ambulance Service. A committee of inquiry established by the Regional Health Authority found those responsible for making the acquisition had made virtually every mistake that could be made in such a process. The final mistake was to put an inadequately tested system into operation without retaining the older manual system as a back up until its reliability had been established. Almost at once the system crashed and the ambulance service descended into chaos. Some patients had to wait hours for an ambulance whilst others were attended by five or six vehicles. Although contemporary media claims that up to thirty deaths resulted have largely been discounted, there can be no doubt that the situation was potentially dangerous. The legally significant question must be whether the failure of the computer system would have caused any death or injury. A relevant decision is that of *R v Poplar Coroner, ex parte Thomas* [1993] 2 All ER 381. Here an asthma sufferer was victim to a severe attack. Attempts were made to summon an ambulance but delays ensured. More than half an hour elapsed before the ambulance arrived by which time the patient had stopped breathing and was certified dead shortly after arrival at hospital. The consultant in charge of the Accident and Emergency Unit at the hospital expressed the opinion that had the patient arrived at the hospital even a few minutes earlier she would not have died.

At issue in the case was the question whether an inquest should be held into the death. The Coroners Act 1988 provided that an inquest was to be held when a patient had died "an unnatural death". The Coroner declined to hold an inquest on the ground that the deceased's death was not unnatural. Although the High Court overturned this ruling, the Court of Appeal agreed with the Coroner. Delivering the judgment of the Court, Dillon LJ held that the cause of the death was the asthma attack. Considering the role played by the late arrival of the ambulance, the judge postulated a number of scenarios which might have been responsible. Delivering his judgment shortly after the failure of the computer system, it is not surprising that one concerned "the failure of a newly installed computer installed by the ambulance service to handle emergency calls more efficiently malfunctioned, as newly installed computers are prone to". In this scenario, he stated, "common sense indicates that what caused the patient's death was ... the asthmatic attack, not the ... malfunction of the computer".

The particular case was concerned with a narrow point and it may be that a causal link could be established between the negligent operation of a computer system and an injury or fatality for the purpose of establishing civil liability. A further incident reported in comp.risks indicates further complexities which may be encountered in the medical field. For a considerable period of time, radiation treatment has been a standard response to forms of cancer. The dosage to be given to a patient is dependent upon a number of variables including the patient's weight. With the previous generation of machine, the operator had to perform the calculations. New equipment was supplied in which the calculations were made automatically. One operator was unaware of this and continued to make the calculations adjusting the machine's output accordingly. The effect of this was that a number of patients received a dosage smaller than the optimum.

It may be that negligence could be ascribed to either producer - for failing to provide adequate documentation or control systems - or to the user for failing to ensure that staff were adequately trained. Given the nature of the incident it may be difficult to establish a causal link. In other reported cases, patients have been given excessive doses of radiation. This clearly would result in physical harm. Underdosing might deprive the patient of some of the benefits of the treatment but would not *per se* cause harm.

Defective Information

In 1988 the United States warship *Vicennes* was on patrol in the Persian Gulf. It was equipped with a state of the art radar system linked to the ship's weapons system. One commentator has said of the system that "it had a lot of information to present to its operator, and cynics charge that it presented it in a form that was cryptic, cluttered and sometimes misleading. An operator saw data he misinterpreted data as a descending aircraft. The aircraft was in fact ascending. This misunderstanding contributed to the perception that the plane was an F-14 on the attack, rather than an Airbus 320 on a commercial route" (Weiner 1993)[3]. The rest is tragic history.

Although the manner in which information was presented to the operator may have been open to criticism, the decision whether to act on it or not remained in human hands. Although there may be a perception that the producers of the system were negligent, the element of human involvement may well be such as to preclude the imposition of property status in respect of the system's output. The same result should apply where expert systems output advice to their users. In a number of instances, however, the possibility of human intervention may be so limited as to make the user effectively a part of the machine. The issue has been discussed in a number of United States cases brought against the Jeppesen Company, an undertaking specialising in the production of charts for use by airline pilots. In a number of instances the information given on the charts was defective and fatal accidents ensued. Liability was imposed under the United States' product liability regime on the basis that a pilot flying at night or in cloud would have no option other than to place total reliance upon the accuracy of the chart. Thus:

> ... although a sheet of paper might not be dangerous, *per se*, it would be difficult indeed to conceive of a saleable commodity with more inherent lethal potential than an aid to aircraft navigation that, contrary to its own design standards, fails to list the highest land mass immediately surrounding a landing site (*Fluor Corp v Jeppesen*, 170 Cal App 3d 468 (1985)).

Given that the Consumer Protection Act provides that the adequacy of any instructions for use supplied with a product are to be taken into account in determining whether it is defective, there seems no good reason why the legislation should not apply where the instructions constitute the product. Instances of this, however, are likely to be few in number. Although there has been a proliferation in the number of expert systems in safety related fields such as engineering and medicine these are invariably intended to be used to provide advice and guidance on a specialised topic to a user who possesses a general level of skill and experience of the subject.

The Development Risks Defence and Computer Software

One of the most controversial aspects of the Consumer Protection Act concerns the provision of a development risks defence. In part the controversy arises from a difference in terminology between the European Directive and the implementing UK legislation. The former provides the producer with a defence where it is established that:

> ... the state of scientific and technical knowledge at the time when he put the product into circulation was not such as to enable the existence of the defect to be established. (Article 7(e))

The Consumer Protection Act provides that the defence is to apply where a producer is able to establish that:

> ... the state of scientific and technical knowledge at the relevant time was not such that a producer of products of the same description as the product in question might have been expected to discover the defect if it had existed in his products while they were under his control ... (section 4(1)(e))

Use of the phrase "might have been expected" appears to render the UK provision more favourable to a producer than the original version. The European Commission at one stage threatened proceedings against the UK Government alleging that the change in terminology constituted a failure fully to implement the provisions of the Directive. To date, no action has ensued.

The question how far the defence (in whatever version) may be relevant in a software context has been the subject of extensive debate. Given the recognition that the state of scientific and technical knowledge does not permit the exhaustive testing of software, some commentators have argued that the defence will be of considerable utility. The contrary view is that a distinction exists between risks whose occurrence was not foreseeable and defects whose existence was undiscoverable. The case of *Smedleys v Breed* [1974] AC 839 provides a helpful illustration of this rather opaque distinction. The appellants had been convicted of an offence under the terms of the Food and Drugs Act 1955. Section 2(1) of this Act prohibited the selling of food which was not of the nature, substance or quality demanded by the purchaser. At issue in the case was a can of peas which contained an unadvertised extra ingredient in the form of a caterpillar (deceased). Liability under the Act was strict but the appellants argued before the House of Lords that they were entitled to the benefit of a statutory defence applying where it could be demonstrated that the presence of the extraneous object "was an unavoidable consequence of the process of collection or preparation" (section 3(3)).

In the year in question, 1971, the appellants had produced some 3,500,000 cans of peas and received only 4 complaints involving the presence of foreign bodies. Extensive checks involving both mechanical devices and human inspection were conducted by them but, presumably owing to a momentary lapse of attention by one of their checkers, the caterpillar escaped discovery. Statistically, the appellants' performance was impressive with a complaint rate of little more than one in a million cans. It was accepted that nothing more could feasibly be done to improve the control system. However, as was stated by Lord Hailsham:

> What has to be shown in order to constitute a defence under section 3(3) of the Act is not that *some* failures are unavoidable and that, owing to the excellence of the system, statistically the failures have been few. This is a matter for mitigation. What has to be shown under section 3(3) is that "the presence of that matter" (i.e., the particular piece of extraneous matter) in the particular parcel of food the subject of the charge was "the unavoidable consequence of the process". As I ventured to point out in the argument, over a long enough run any sort of process,

however excellent, will statistically result in some failures, human or otherwise, and these are statistically predictable in the light of experience. But that will not necessarily be a defence under section 3(3).

In the case of software it is the vast number of possible interactions which defeats any attempt at exhaustive testing rather than the intrinsic difficulty of the task of identifying a particular defect. A further argument may also be advanced against the application of the development risks defence. To an extent greater than with any other product, software is a creation of the human mind. Any defects are introduced by its creator(s). It would appear contrary to the aims of the legislation to allow a party to be allowed both to create a defect and subsequently claim that this was unforeseeable.

Non-Contractual Liability

There will be many situations when the Consumer Protection Act will be of little relevance. It may be that the damage caused falls outside the somewhat narrow boundaries established by the statute. It may also be that the damage resulted from the act or omission of someone other than a producer. The following section will consider the rights and remedies which may exist when parties are in a contractual relationship. Initially, however, consideration will be given to the application of principles of non-contractual liability.

In order to establish liability under the law of tort/delict a pursuer is generally required to establish that the defender was negligent. The basis for this may lie either in an act or an omission. Two candidates may be identified for the role of defender. First consideration will be given to the liability of a producer or supplier of software and, second, to the liability of a party using (or failing to use) software in the course of their work.

A Reasonable Software Producer?

The concept of the "reasonable man" is one of the most famous creations of the common law. A defender will be liable if he or she failed to display the level of skill and care reasonably to be expected of them. The value of the concept lies in part in its flexibility. Effectively, individuals will be judged by the standards of their peers. Such an approach can be of maximum effectiveness in the case of an established profession or activity. In the present context, the question "what would a reasonable software producer (or supplier) do?" has to be prefaced by that of "Who is a software producer?" Although a number of professional bodies such as the British Computer Society operate in the area, these lack the status of the regulatory bodies associated with the older professions such as law, accountancy and medicine.

Liability for Use or Non-Use of Software

Is too much faith placed in simulated models rather than human observation?

A common issue in debate on the use of and failures in safety critical software systems is the aleged over dependence of human operators on the computer elements. An example recently cited concerned an experiment conducted on subjects who, without their knowledge, were given specially programmed calculators, then told to compute a few simple sums. The results indicated that most people trusted the machine even when a simple mental calculation would have given a different and correct answer. The experiment raises interesting questions concerning the possibility of such attitudes prevailing even in the highest levels of science. Is it wise to allow computer modelling to replace human observation? Of course, it is widely accepted that the use of new technology is essential if scientific advances are to be made. It has been said that the development of the Space Shuttle would not have been possible without Computer Aided Engineering. Bearing this in mind, what standards are to be expected of those who design or engineer systems which may be safety critical and how does the law apportion liability?

Of course a decision to adopt an innovative technique, as yet not extensively used, in itself will rarely be classed as negligence, but special care must be given to its application. If the innovative technique fails, and it is established that no reasonable member of that profession would have employed such a method, then the use of such a technique may be judged to be negligent.

Could it be considered negligent not to use new technology?

Although the use of new technology always carries a certain degree of risk, it may well be that overall the level of risk is reduced. The system may be safer, although not totally risk free, if designed by new technology and by the application of new methods. Bearing this in mind, might it ever be considered negligent *not* to use a computer based technology? A number of earlier cases concerned with the shipping industry and its relationship with new technology provide useful parallels with the use of computers and computer simulated models.

In the case of *T J Hooper* 60 F 2d 737 (1932), two barges were lost at sea partly because their tugs had not been equipped with working radio receivers. If radios had been installed, it would have been possible to listen to weather forecasts thus enabling them to seek shelter from the storm. At that time the installation of radios on tugs was not common practice. In spite of this, the owners were held to be negligent on the basis that "a whole calling may have unduly lagged in the adoption of new and available services".

However in the case of *United States Fire Insurance Co v United States* 806 F.2d 1529 (1987), Coast Guards who failed to identify the location of a hazard to navigation, were held not to be negligent even although it was agreed that an available computerised method was superior in its accuracy to the manual technique actually used by the coast guards. At an earlier stage, a court had found the Coast Guard to be negligent by not marking the position of the wreckage correctly but the Appeal Court held that the Coast Guard was not under an absolute duty to mark wreckage, but only to exercise due care in searching for it. The point was made that

> ...the district court must consider what actually transpired, not simply against what would have transpired [had the marker been in the correct location] but rather against what probably would have occurred had the Coast Guard exercised due care.

The fact that the desired result (in light of hindsight) did not occur does not imply that reasonable skill and care was not used, nor is it sufficient merely to establish that a new method which could have been adopted is superior to the old method. It must be established that in the circumstances, the risk was identifiable, that the failure to adopt the new method or the new technology was in itself a breach of a duty of care and that in the absence of such a breach, the loss or injury would not have occurred.

The likelihood of establishing negligence may depend on the extent to which the use of the new technology would have minimised the risk of loss or injury. Would use of the new technology have been very likely to have prevented such an error, or would it merely have reduced the risk but not eliminated it ? Of course such questions can only be resolved after the event on the basis of available expert evidence.

However, it should be said that manufacturer and designers must endeavour to keep themselves informed of new technical developments, as it is possible that a failure to adopt a new method could be considered negligent if an injury or loss occurred which would have been very unlikely to have occurred had the new technology been employed. Judging by *T J Hooper*, this may apply even if the use of such technology is not yet standard practice. Failure to respond to an identifiable risk may well be considered to be negligent.

Software Can Damage Your Wealth - Aspects of Contractual Liability

In the situation where the operation of software or a software based product has resulted in injury or damage an action may lie in delict or under the provisions of the Consumer Protection Act. The latter statute offers no remedy when loss is economic in nature whilst the availability of compensation for economic loss in the law of delict has been severely restricted by recent decisions of the House of Lords. In the situation where the complaint relates to the quality of the performance of software the only realistic prospect of success lies under the law of contract.

Once again, the issue of the status of software may be a matter of some significance. If the transaction is regarded as involving goods (whether a sale or other form of transfer) the implied terms of conformity with description, merchantable quality and fitness for purpose will apply with the supplier being held strictly liable for any defects in the goods supplied. If software should be regarded as a species of service, the supplier will be held strictly liable in respect of any goods supplied. In respect of the service component, however, the supplier will be required only to exercise of reasonable skill and care with liability being imposed only if negligence can be established.

In determining the distinction between these two species of contract, two distinct lines of judicial authority can be identified. In the case of *Lee v Griffin* (1861) 1 B&S 272, the Court of Appeal was faced with a contract under which a dentist undertook to make a set of dentures for a patient. A dispute subsequently arising, the court was faced *inter alia* with the question of the contract's proper categorisation. Holding the contract to be one of sale, the court held that the essential criteria was whether anything that could be the subject matter of a sale had come into existence. In the event, for example, that an attorney was engaged to draw up a deed for a client, it was held that the contract would be one for services. In other situations, however:

> I do not think that the test to apply to these cases is whether the value of the work exceeds that of the materials used in its execution; for, if a sculptor were employed to execute a work of art, greatly as his skill and labour, assuming it to be of the highest description, might exceed the value of the marble on which he worked, the contract would in my opinion, nevertheless be a contract for the sale of a chattel.

Although it might be argued that any piece of tangible property must have some intrinsic value, however small, it would appear that this test requires that the product have some significant resale value in its own rather than in a representative capacity.

The distinction between sale of goods and supply of services was again at issue before the Court of Appeal in the case of *Robinson* v *Graves* [1935] 1 KB 579. The contract here was one whereby an artist agreed to paint a portrait of his client's wife. On the basis of the situation hypothesised in *Lee v Griffin* it would appear that such a transaction should be regarded as one of sale. In the event, however, it was held that it should be regarded as one for services. In reaching this conclusion the Court sought to identify the prime purpose of the contract. In the oft quoted words of Greer LJ:

> If the substance of the contract ... is that skill and labour have to be exercised for the production of the article and ... it is only ancillary to that that there will pass from the artist to his client or customer some materials in addition to the skill involved in the production of the portrait, that does not make any difference to the result, because the substance of the contract is the skill and experience of the artist in producing the picture.

Although the court in *Robinson v Graves* did not overrule, or even distinguish, the earlier authority it must be doubted how far the two approaches can truly be considered compatible. In attempting to consider further the basis of the distinction between goods and services, a measure of assistance may be obtained from the United States' authority of *Barbee v Rogers* 425 SW 2d 342 (1968). Here, a firm of opticians advertised the provision of contact lenses at a fixed charge. One customer suffered eye damage, allegedly as a result of the provision of unsuitable lenses, and brought an action under the relevant sale of goods legislation. Holding that the transaction should be characterised as one for services it was held that although a uniform price was charged for contact lenses the amount of attention required by each customer would vary as would the prescription for the individual sets of lenses. Although this notion of the contract for services representing a unique relationship between the provider and the receiver cannot provide a single infallible test as to the status of the transaction it will hold true in many cases. In the event, for example, that a customer contracts with a photographic processing laboratory with a view to his film being developed and printed, this transaction may be one of hundreds or even thousands entered into by the laboratory on that day. All of these films will be subjected to identical processes within the laboratory, yet each contract will be unique in that every customer must receive his own film back and the contract will be one for services. The converse proposition may be more certain. Where identical items are produced and sold without modification, regardless of the amount of labour exerted in the production process, the ultimate transaction must be regarded as one of sale.

Much legal ink has been consumed in discussion of the question whether software should be regarded as a product or a service. On occasion the discussion proceeds from the false premise that there is a single type of software. In reality, three basic types may be identified. In many large-scale software contracts, a party is contracted to produce a single version of a computer program for the exclusive use of a single customer. Such a transaction seems to fit most naturally into the services category. At the opposite end of the software spectrum is standard software. This will include application packages such as spread sheet or word processing programs produced for use on personal computers. By the criteria identified above, these should be regarded as involving goods. Somewhere in between comes a category referred to as customised software. This sees a standard program being modified to suit the needs of a specific customer and may be an area which is not susceptible of precise categorisation.

In many situations a contract will relate to the provision of a computer system containing a mixture of hardware and software. In such cases there appears no doubt that the transaction will be regarded as one for goods. When discussion has occurred concerning the status of software in isolation the view has generally been taken that it was not necessary to determine the point. Thus, in the case of *Eurodynamic Systems v General Automation* (Queens Bench Division, 6 September 1988), Steyn J after surveying a number of United States authorities suggesting that software should be regarded as goods, stated that "the decision on this point is not of critical importance". It is well established that the requirements of merchantability and fitness for purpose are not generally to be interpreted as requiring that a product be perfect. In the case of software, it was stated:

> ... the expert evidence convincingly showed that it is regarded as acceptable practice to supply computer programmes (*sic*) (including system software) that

contain errors and bugs. The basis of the obligation is that, pursuant to his obligation (free or chargeable as the case may be), the supplier will correct errors and bugs that prevent the product from being properly used. Not every bug or error in a computer programme (*sic*) can therefore be characterised as a breach of contract.

Similar views were expressed by Staughton LJ in the case of *Saphena Computing Ltd v Allied Collection Agencies Ltd* (Court of Appeal, 3 May 1989). This case concerned a contract for the provision of software. The software was installed between September 1985 and February 1986. By 11th February 1986 it remained incapable of functioning in a satisfactory manner, and in a telephone conversation between the parties it was agreed that the contract relationship should be terminated. The issues to be resolved in the legal proceedings under discussion concerned, *inter alia*, the customer's claim for compensation on the ground that the software supplied was not reasonably fit for its purpose. Delivering the judgement of the Court of Appeal, Staughton LJ held that it was:

> ... common ground that the law governing these contracts was precisely the same whether they were contracts for the sale of goods or the supply of services. It is therefore unnecessary to consider into which category they might come. But it is important to remember that software is not a commodity which is handed over or delivered once and for all at one time. It may well have to be tested and modified as necessary. It would not be a breach of contract at all to deliver software in the first instance with a bug in it.

Although it was accepted that the software was not in an acceptable condition on the date when the contract was terminated, it was held to be part of the contract that the suppliers should have the "right and the duty to test and modify as necessary the software they supplied". The customer's over-hasty action in terminating the contract deprived the supplier of their right and relieved them from their duty to modify the software.

Similar issues arose in *Simpson Nash Wharton v Barco Graphics Ltd* (Queens Bench Division, 1 July 1991). In this case, the plaintiffs had agreed to purchase a hardware and software from the defendants for use in the design of packaging for food, drink and pharmaceutical products. The system, which was a new version of an existing product, was delivered on 20th June. Despite many complaints and much work by the suppliers over the following months it failed to function in a satisfactory fashion and on 27th October the plaintiffs' solicitors wrote to the defendants giving notice they were rejecting the system and seeking compensation.

The time scale involved in this case was broadly similar to that in *Saphena*. The defendants, whilst not claiming that the system was operating in a satisfactory manner and even conceding that the plaintiffs might justifiably have rejected the system shortly after delivery. They alleged that by retaining the system beyond the middle of July, the plaintiffs must be deemed to have accepted it. Support for this contention was sought from the decision of the High Court in the case of *Bernstein v Pamson Motors* [1987] 2 All ER 220. In this case, the passage of a period of 3-4 weeks was held sufficient to prevent the purchaser of a new car from rejecting what was accepted to be an unmerchantable vehicle. Whilst Judge Rivlin accepted *Bernstein* as authority for the proposition that the determination what was a reasonable time for the buyer to examine goods with a view to discovering any defects was dictated by the nature of the goods rather than by that of a particular defect, he held that:

> ... the goods in this case were highly sophisticated goods which required a deal of training to understand and work them satisfactorily, and moreover they were goods which were being constantly developed and improved by the provision of new software and the like.

Although the plaintiffs succeeded in the present case, the dilemma facing customers is apparent and the position may be considerably less satisfactory in the situation where a software defect manifests itself only after a significant period of time. As the case of *Bernstein* indicates, of course, problems are by no means confined to the software sector.

The most recent decision concerning the status of and liability for software under the existing legislation is that of *St Albans District Council v ICL*, 3 October 1994, Queens Bench Division (*The Times*, 4 October 1994). The defendant company supplied the Council (and many other local authorities) with software to be used to administer the community charge regime. Amongst its functions, the software calculated how many residents would be liable to pay the charge in each area. Owing to an error in the software, the number of taxpayers was overstated. This resulted in the charge being levied at a level insufficient to generate the required income for the Council, the shortfall being estimated at £1,314,846.

Holding the defendant liable for this sum, Scott Baker J stated that the transaction was regulated by the Sale of Goods Act. This conclusion was based upon a study of the status of software under tax law, it being commented that if software was not a good, it was difficult to see what it was. The importance of the application of the Sale of Goods Act lay in the fact that the defendant had sought to limit the extent of its liability contractually to £100,000. Under the provisions of the Unfair Contract Terms Act 1977, any attempt to restrict or exclude the application of the implied terms of merchantability and fitness for purpose will succeed only if this can satisfy the statutory criterion of reasonableness. This was held not to be the case. The parties were not considered to enjoy equal bargaining power. The Council was faced with a statutory requirement to implement the system, and because of the Council's previous investment in hardware, ICL were effectively monopoly suppliers. Also taken into account was the fact that the defendant was insured for losses of up to £50 million, and was in a position to pass on the premium cost to its customers.

There is before Parliament at the time of writing the Sale and Supply of Goods Bill, under which it is proposed to replace the venerable term "merchantable quality" with a requirement that goods be of "satisfactory quality". This term is defined as encompassing freedom from minor defects, safety, durability, appearance and finish. It is arguable that this provision simply restates factors which are currently taken into account by the courts; but the specific reference to freedom from minor defects may prompt a measure of concern on the part of software producers and vendors.

Conclusions

The cases heard so far are of limited precedential value, indicated by the fact that so few have found a place in the Law Reports. In every case, the contracts have been for comparatively large scale projects - the contract in *Simpson Nash Wharton* was costed at some £206,000. With only the one exception discussed above, the courts have avoided giving a direct answer to the question whether software is a product or a service, in large part because the negotiations leading up to the conclusion of fairly major contracts have allowed them to claim that they are merely interpreting the terms of the particular bargain between the parties. The issues may have to be addressed more directly if and when disputes concerning smaller scale, possibly consumer, contracts involving standard software are litigated. It would appear from the cases decided to date that at least some functional requirements will be implied into any contract and consideration will require to be given to the interpretation of the famous concepts of merchantable quality and fitness for purpose.

Standard software packages are invariably supplied with a licence, generally referred to as shrink wrap licences. The term dates back to the early days of home computers when programs, normally in the form of games, were supplied on cassette tapes and the terms of a basic licence were printed on the cellophane wrapping. Today, the licence is normally buried inside the packaging. A typical approach is for the licence to be printed on the outside of an envelope in which are contained the program disks. A statement is normally printed to the effect that opening the envelope will constitute acceptance of the terms of the licence.

It is extremely questionable whether the terms of such a licence can ever be considered binding on a customer. The contract with the supplier will normally have been concluded some time before the packaging is opened and the terms of the licence revealed. The licence will therefore represent a unilateral attempt by the supplier to impose new terms and conditions. On the authority of the English case of *Thornton v Shoe Lane Parking* [1971] 2 QB 163, it may confidently be asserted that such techniques will not be accepted by the courts. A further complication is that the software may be supplied by an intermediary retailer whilst the licence is issued by a producer. In this situation there will be no contractual relationship between the licensor and potential licensee.

The licence itself may normally be divided into two sections. The first appears rather user friendly and will confer rights to use the software in specified ways and to make back up copies. Although the implementation of the European Union Directive has enhanced the statutory rights of a software user, these are still limited especially in relation to the making of back up copies. Such benefits come at a price for the user. The second element of the licence invariably seeks to exclude liability for any loss or damage suffered as

a result of a defect in the software. Although the trend appears to be towards a more limited form of exclusion, until very recently one of the market's leading word processor packages sought to exclude liability to make even a refund of the purchase price in the event that a fault on the disk supplied rendered the software unusable.

To an extent, the reluctance on the part of software suppliers to accept responsibility for losses resulting from its operation may not be unreasonable. To an extent greater than with other products, software may be used in a great variety of circumstances. An incident has been reported, for example, of a heart surgeon using a standard spreadsheet package to analyse data relating to patients in the course of an operation. Any error in the program could have fatal consequences. Even in its "normal" field of operation, a spreadsheet may be used for household accounts or to prepare a bid for a multi-million pound contract. Unlike the situation applying in cases such as *Saphena* where the software was "not delivered once, only once and once and for all" there is little prospect of errors being corrected on an individual basis, although the offer of free or reduced price upgrades of the software may be considered somewhat analogous. The question whether software is defective will have to be determined largely by reference to the state in which it was delivered. Even assuming the application of the Sale of Goods Act, perfection is seldom to be equated with merchantability, whilst applications such as those described above might be regarded as special purposes requiring notice be given to the supplier as a condition for the application of the implied term of fitness for purpose.

The conclusion may be that the application of the implied terms of merchantability and fitness for purpose in the context of standard software will not prove ruinous to software producers and suppliers. It may be that attempts to exclude liability may be more perilous. The operation of the Unfair Contract Terms Act renders invalid any attempt to restrict or exclude the application of the implied terms of the Sale of Goods Act in the case of consumer contracts and subjects these to the application of a test of reasonableness in other cases. Further, the Consumer Transactions (Restrictions on Statements) Order 1976 renders criminal the mere attempt to invoke such clauses.

Chapter Six

Conclusion

One of the landmark events in history was the discovery how to make clay pots and containers. This breakthrough meant that it became possible to move foods and liquids and to store them safe from the vagaries of the weather. Paradoxically, the act of confining a product within a container served to increase its mobility and utility. A similar phenomenon can be seen operating in many aspects of human development. The dissemination of knowledge was increased dramatically when technology permitted thoughts and ideas to be "captured" in writing. The steam engine harnesses and controls the power of steam within a physical structure.

As described in previous chapters, the most significant effect of the "computer revolution" has been to free information from the physical ties that were previously required to afford it practical utility and financial value. The societal impact may well be as profound as that following from the invention of pottery or, more recently, the steam engine. Possession of information becomes a matter of little significance with the key determinant of wealth and power being concerned with the extent of access to information.

Up to the present, the law has tended to focus on the vessel rather than the contents. Even in areas such as copyright, the requirement for a linkage between information and a storage medium is to be seen with protection commencing only when the information is recorded in some material form. In other areas, containment of an intangible serves to confer a new and more extensive legal status. The air cannot be owned, but when it is contained in a car tyre any deliberate release may be prosecuted as a form of damage to property.

It would, of course, be misleading to suggest that electronic information is freed totally from physical confines. There will always remain need for information to be recorded initially in some place and on some storage device. From there, however, it may be "delivered" anywhere in the world without the need for any tangible container. An increasing number of books are now available for "downloading" *via* the *Internet.* Software may also be supplied in the same manner. In such a situation, there would appear to be no role for the Sale of Goods Act as presently constituted.

When the word "revolution" is used in its social and political sense, the image is normally of tumult and chaos and tumbrils rumbling towards the guillotine. The imagery of the industrial revolution is of smoke and steam and noise. The information revolution is both quieter and yet more pervasive.

Information and knowledge have been regarded as exclusively human qualities, and it is a mark of the impact of the information technology revolution that machines are now performing the tasks that used to be associated with the human mind. It is machines rather than humans which are responsible for adding value to information, with "expert" systems operating in domains which were previously the exclusive province of professionals such as lawyers, engineers and accountants. From both a social and a legal perspective, the change is at a qualitatively greater level than that produced by the industrial revolution. That served to increase, albeit dramatically, physical capabilities and the value of physical assets such as coal and iron ore. Transport remained transport, however, and the increase in value of the raw materials posed no conceptual problems for legal structures used to fluctuations in commodity values.

The information age has fewer precedents and many traditional legal models are ill suited to serve as the basis for lasting regulation. Fault lines are most apparent in respect of the concepts of property and ownership. Whilst flexibility is a virtue in enabling to law to accommodate change, excessive flexibility deprives its subject of any coherent structure or form. The adaptability of legal concepts such as copyright and sale has provided valuable breathing space. Ad hoc legislation epitomised by measures such as the Data Protection and Computer Misuse Acts has proved of limited value. The urgent legal task as we approach the millennium is to devote time and effort in order to devise structures and concepts that will afford due recognition to the realities of the information age.

This work began with a study of the impact of the computer revolution upon concepts of individual privacy. It may be appropriate to give the last word to the first holder of the Office of Data Protection Registrar, Mr Eric Howe. In his final report before retiring from the position he surveyed developments in computing and concluded:

> So, whither the dream and whither the nightmare? The dream is racing towards reality ... the present world of computing - with its sophisticated data collection devices, its massive data banks and its burgeoning computer facilities - shows the dream taking place all around us. The nightmare increasingly disturbs our sleep. (Tenth Report of the Data Protection Registrar, June 1994)

The challenge may be as much for the concept of national sovereignty as for individual rights. Much is written today about the *Internet*. Originally devised in the 1970s as a means of distributing the United States military's computing facilities to guard against the risk of nuclear attack, the system is now accessed by some 16 million people world-wide. Using the general telecommunications infrastructure, use of the system is virtually uncontrollable. Definition of the *Internet* and other computer-based networks is a difficult task. Convergence of technologies means that the differences between telecommunications, broadcasting and even the press have become so blurred as to be almost invisible. As has been discussed extensively in the context of computer pornography, moving images of a technical quality at least equal to that of a television broadcast may be transmitted over a computer network. No national system of control can have more than a marginal effect. The urgent need is for a vastly increased degree of international consensus in all areas of the law. Like the corner shop faced with the competition of the superstore, the day of the national legal system may be approaching its end.

Notes

Chapter One: Crime and the Computer

1. UNIX is a registered trade mark of AT&T Laboratories.
2. Female 'hackers' do seem to be rarer than their male counterparts although according to Hacker folklore, 'hacker' marriages are common with romance blossoming online. Leslie Lynne Doucette who in 1990, admitted trafficking in stolen telephone access codes and who was the head of an extensive computer fraud scheme is one of the few reported female 'hacker' cases.
3. Fire Walls are designed to regulate traffic both entering and exiting sites. All outgoing and incoming packets to and from the Internet are examined, often only packets from registered sources are permitted to enter.
4. Gopher is a shared protocol on the Internet which allows any site running a gopher client to browse the public domain information available at any Internet site running a gopher server. The gopher software was developed by the University of Minnesota whose state emblem is a gopher. The term was also chosen as the gopher appears to be 'burrowing' across Cyberspace and dragging back a compendium of information resources and presenting them in a common menu.
5. The Internet Underground which contains a link to the Boxing Page which lists the function of all the colour boxes and describes how to build them!
6. World Wide Web is the successor to Gopher. Developed by CERN in Switzerland, information sources on the Internet can be accessed via hypertext browsers, thus greatly enhancing the ease with which users can navigate the information highways. Gopher sites are linked to the Web which is quickly emerging as the standard information server on the Internet. 'Hacking' the Web is a hot topic for discussion on the Net News. Fears as to its security are also quickly emerging!
7. Browsers such as Mosaic and Cello offer a high level, hypertext-linked interface to the information resources of the Internet.
8. File Transfer Protocol is the precursor to Gopher. This shared protocol allowed sites to exchange files across a common platform. Many sites permit anonymous login to the public domain areas.
9. In his paper "The Internet Worm: An Analysis", (spaf@cs.purdue.edu), Eugene Spafford commented that many programmers could have written the worm with far fewer errors, and that had it been 'properly' written it could have ben considerably more virulent.

10. These viruses may lie dormant in a computer for some time and come into operation only when the computer's internal clock indicates that the date is Friday 13th or March 6th, Michaelangelo's birthday.

11. Both Law Commissions have considered computer crime. The first steps were taken by the Scottish Law Commission which published a Consultative Memorandum (No 68) in 1986, and followed this with a Report in 1987. The Law Commission, arguing that the title "computer crime" was excessively conclusory since significant aspects of computer-related conduct might not constitute an offence under existing provisions of the criminal law, published a Working Paper (No 110) in 1988 and a Report (No 186) in 1989.

12. The Audit Commission has conducted triennial surveys since 1980 which attempt to assess the scale first of computer fraud and, in its latest report, of other forms of computer abuse. The Commission's statistics can only reflect those instances of fraud and abuse reported by their victims, but do provide a counterpoint to some of the wilder speculations published in the media about the cost of computer crime.

13. In the case of *United States v Lambert* 446 F Supp 890 (1978), the defendant sold information derived from a computer owned by the Drug Enforcement Agency, which identified informants and described the status of the agency's investigations. No tangible property was removed, but the District Court upheld the competence of a prosecution alleging theft of "any record, voucher, money or thing of value to the United States" (18 USC s 641), holding that the conjunction of the terms "record" and "thing of value" extended the application of the provision beyond the situation where physical property was removed.

Chapter Two: The Individual in the Computer Society

1. Retention of details of telephone numbers called is a recent phenomonen. Prior to the introduction of digital telephone exchanges, a record was maintained only of units consumed. For a description of practices in telephone billing see P Fitzgerald and M Leopold, *Strangers on the Line* (Bodley Head, 1987).

2. S A Baker, *Don't Worry Be Happy*, Wired 2.06. Wired is one of the growing number of 'on-line' journals available on the *Internet*. A number of references will be made to such sources throughout this text.

3. See the Report of the Committee on Data Protection (1978: Cmnd 7431) where the comment is made that "... it is now official Swedish policy to establish a central register of personal information covering all Swedish residents. This central register will be public and will show each resident's income as well as his name, personal number, address and nationality. In the UK by contrast, it is generally the case that the privacy of a person's financial circumstances is jealously guarded ... As one member of the new Swedish data protection commission is reported to have said, "I know

that if you tell an Englishman that he can't keep his income secret from his wife, he thinks he has nothing left to lose but Swedes are quite happy to ... (have the information publicly available)" (para 4.05) Perhaps less seriously, it is reported that when the pop group ABBA were at the height of their fame, requests from their fans for copies of their tax returns (which included a photograph) swamped the Swedish tax system.

4.   Such issues were raised during the 1980s when the United States-owned *Lexis* system took over and closed down the competing United Kingdom-owned system *Eurolex*.

Chapter Three: Elements of Data Protection

1.   The Committee's deliberations spanned a general election and a change of governing party. Requests by the Committee to both the appointing Labour and the incoming Conservative governments to expand its terms of reference to include the public sector were rejected.

2.   Much of the legislation also applies to the operations of computer bureaux - those who make computing services available to others. The scope of this definition is broader than might initially appear to be the case. A party will be classed as operating a computer bureau if they enter into an agreement to allow another to use their facilities for the processing of personal data on an occasional basis. In the event that two undertakings enter into an agreement permitting use of each other's computing facilities in the event of a breakdown, both will be classed as operating a computer bureau.

3.   A perhaps optimistic assumption. See Chapter Five for information regarding instances of software malfunctions.

Chapter Four: Intellectual Property and the Computer

1.   Implementation of the European Union Directive in 1995 will extend this period to 70 years *post mortem*. Only one work benefits from what is effectively perpetual copyright. Rights in the play *Peter Pan* were bequeathed by its author J E Barrie to Great Ormond Street Childrens' Hospital and royalties from its performances constitute a significant portion of the hospital's income. At the time the Copyright Designs and Patents Bill was before Parliament, the 50th anniversary of the author's death was approaching and, following extensive lobbying, a not inappropriate amendment was made to ensure that the work's copyright, like its major character, would never grow old. Discounting its *sui generis* protection, the example of Peter Pan illustrates what may be a difficult situation arising from the implementation of the European Union Directive. Copyright would have expired in 1987 only to be resurrected in 1995 for a further 12-year period. The works of a number of other authors such as James Joyce will also fall into this category.

2. These figures are based on calculations made by the Business Software Alliance and reported at the conference *Computer Law and Business* organised by the Society for Computers and Law and held in Bath in June 1994.
3. Although only a single word was involved, the case report indicates that considerable time and effort went into its devising. Following anti-trust litigation in the United States, the Standard Oil Corporation had to devise a new brand name for its petroleum products. The word Exxon was selected in part as having no meaning in any known language and being readily pronounceable by people of every tongue. It is used in almost every country in the world although, despite the litigation being brought before the English courts, the brand name Esso is applied in the United Kingdom.
4. In the United States case of *Trust Company Bank v The Putnam Publishing Group, Inc* 5 USPQ 2d (BNA) 1874 (1988), the owners of the copyright in *Gone with the Wind* unsuccessfully argued that copyright had been infringed by a second novel *The Blue Bicycle*. Although this was set in France during the Second World War, it was alleged that it was "a mere transposition of the characters and events from Georgia during the Civil War to France during World War II".

Chapter Five: Liability Issues

1. Most of the examples of software failure cited in this chapter have been culled from the columns of comp.risks, an *Internet* based newsgroup which chronicles the failures of safety critical systems and the risks they pose to the public.
2. Proposals for a second Directive which would have implemented a broadly similar regime within the services sector were submitted by the Commission in 1990. The proposals were withdrawn for amendment following the adoption of the doctrine of 'subsidiarity'. It appears unlikely that the Directive will be re-introduced in the foreseeable future.
3. In fact, the plane was an Airbus A 300 rather than the controversial computer-controlled A 320.

Bibliography

Books

Bowcott, O., and Hamilton, S., *Beating the System*, Bloomsbury, 1990

Buchanan, B. A., *The Power of the Machine*, Viking, 1992.

Chalton, S., and Gaskill, S., (Eds) *The Encyclopaedia of Data Protection Law*, Sweet and Maxwell, 1988.

Cornish, W. R., *Intellectual Property* (2nd Edition), Sweet and Maxwell, 1989.

Cornwall, H., *Datatheft,* Heinemann, 1987.

Cornwall, H., *The Computer Hacker's Handbook,* Century , 1986.

Dern, D. P., *The Internet Guide for New Users*, McGraw Hill, 1994.

Fitzgerald, P., and Leopold, M., and P., *Stranger on the Line*, The Bodley Head, 1987.

Hondius, F., *Emerging Data Protection in Europe*, North Holland, 1975.

Lehmann, M., and Tapper C., (eds), *A Handbook of European Software Law*, Oxford University Press, 1993.

Lloyd, I., *Information Technology Law*, Butterworths, 1993.

MacQueen, H. L., *Copyright, Competition and Industrial Design*, Aberdeen University Press, 1989.

Miller, A., The *Assault on Privacy*, Ann Arbor 1970.

Meijboom A. P., and Prins C., (Eds), *The Law of Information Technology in Europe 1992*, Kluwer 1991

Pelton, J., *Global Talk*, Harvester Press, 1981.

Raymond, E. S., *The New Hacker's Dictionary* (2nd Edition), MIT Press, 1993.

Reed C., (Ed), *Computer Law* (2nd Edition), Blackstone, 1993.

Rheingold, H., *Virtual Reality*, Seeker and Warburg, 1991.

Saxby, S., *The Age of Information*, Macmillan, 1990.

Saxby, S., (Ed), *The Encyclopaedia of Information Technology Law*, Sweet and Maxwell, 1990

Sieber, U., *The International Computer Crime Handbook*, Wiley, 1986.

Sieber, U., *The International Emergence of Criminal Information Law*, Heymanns, 1992.

Stair Memorial Encyclopaedia of the Laws of Scotland. Volume 19, Part II *Intellectual Property*.

Stoll, C., *The Cuckoo's Egg,* The Bodley Head, 1990.

Tapper, C., *Computer Law* (4th Edition), Longman, 1989.

Wacks, R., *Personal Information: Privacy and the Law,* Clarendon Press, 1989.

Wasik, M., *Crime and the Computer*, Clarendon Press, 1990.

Westin, A., *Privacy and Freedom*, Bodley Head, 1970.

Wiener, L. R., *Digital Woes*, Addison Wesley, 1993.

Reports

Report of the Committee on Data Protection. Cmnd 7431, 1978.

Report of the Committee on Privacy. Cmnd 5012, 1972.

Computers and Privacy, Cmnd 6353, 1975.

Computers: Safeguards for Privacy, Cmnd 6354, 1975.

Computer Software and Intellectual Property. Congress of the United States Office of Technology Assessment.

Computer Crime, Scottish Law Commission Consultative Memorandum No 68 (1986) and Report (Cm 174) 1987.

Computer Misuse, Law Commission Working Paper No 110 (1988) and Report No 186 (1989).

Computer Pornography, Home Affairs Committee, Session 1993-4, First Report..

Computer Related Crime, Council of Europe, 1989.

Computer Related Crime. Analysis of Legal Policy, Organisation for Economic Co-operation and Development, 1986.

Copyright and the Challenge of Technology, Commission of the European Communities, 1988

Data Protection, Cmnd 8539, 1982.

Data Protection Controls and Safeguards, Report by the Comptroller and Auditor General, 1993.

New Technologies: A Challenge to Privacy Protection?, Council of Europe, 1989.

Survey of Computer Fraud and Abuse, The Audit Commission for Local Authorities and the National Health Service in England and Wales, 1982, 1985, 1987, 1991.

Reports of the Data Protection Registrar , 1985-1994. HMSO.

Articles

August, R., *Corpus Juris Roboticum,* 8 Computer/Law Journal (1988) 375

Bainbridge, D., *Hacking - The Unauthorised Access of Computer Systems; The Legal Implications,* 52 Modern Law Review (1989) 236.

Benn M. N., and Superfine, R. J., *Disablement of Software Risks and Potential Liabilities,* 6 Software Law Journal (1993) 11.

Bing, J., *Reflections on a Data Protection Policy for 1992,* 5 Yearbook of Law, Computers and Technology (1991) 164.

Blume, P., *An EEC Policy for Data Protection,* 11 Computer/Law Journal (1992) 399.

Brannigan V. M., and Dayhoff, R. E., *Liability for Personal Injures Caused by Defective Medical Computer Programs,* 7 American Journal of Law and Medicine (1981) 123.

Brannigan, V. M., *The Regulation of Medical Expert Computer Software as a "Device" Under the Food, Drug and Cosmetic Act,* 27 Jurimetrics Journal(1987) 370.

Breyer, S., *The Uneasy Case for Copyright; A study of Copyright in Books, Photocopies and Computer Programs,* 84 Harvard Law review (1970) 282.

Burkert, H., *Institutions of Data Protection - An Attempt at a Functional Explanation of European National Data Protection Laws,* 3 Computer/Law Journal (1981) 167.

Charlesworth, A., *Legislating Against Computer Misuse: The Trials and Tribulations of the UK Computer Misuse Act 1990,* 4 Journal of Law and Information Science (1993) 80.

Curtis, W., *Engineering Computer "Look and Feel"*, 30 Jurimetrics Journal (989) 51.

Effross, W. E., *Assessing Computer Associates v. Altai: How Will the "Golden Nugget" Test Pan Out?*, 19 Rutgers Computer and Technology Law Journal (1993) 1.

Forester, T., and Morrison, P., *Computer Unreliability and Social Vulnerability*, 1990 Futures 462.

Gemignani, M., *Product Liability and Software*, 8 Rutgers Computer and Technology Law Journal (1981) 173.

Hall, D., *Strict Products Liability and Computer Software:* Caveat Vendor, 4 Computer/Law Journal (1983) 373.

Grant Hammond, R., *Theft of Information*, 100 Law Quarterly Review (1984) 252.

Grant Hammond, R., *Electronic Crime in Canadian Courts*, 6 Oxford Journal of Legal Studies (1986) 145.

Hogg, M. A., *The Very Private Life of Privacy*, 2(3) Hume Papers on Public Policy (1994) 1.

Hemnes, T. M. N., *Three Common Fallacies in the User Interface Copyright Debate*, Computer Law and Practice (1990) 163.

Liebman, K., *Untying the Knot, Computer law and the New Technologies*, 1 International Journal of Law and Information Technology (1993) 225.

Lloyd, I., *Computer Abuse and the Law*, 104 Law Quarterly Review (1988) 202.

Lloyd, I., *Data Protection: Little Brother Fights Back?* 48 Modern Law Review (1985) 190.

Lloyd, I., *Privacy, Data Protection and the Poll Tax*, 1988 Scots Law Times 264.

Lloyd, I., *Liability for Defective Software.*, 32 Reliability Engineering and System Safety (1991) 193.

MacQueen, H. L., *Extending Intellectual Property: Producers v. Users*, 45 Northern Ireland Legal Quarterly (1994) 30.

Maule, M., *Applying Strict Products Liability to Computer Software*, 27 Tulsa Law Journal (1992) 735.

Meadow, R., *Television Formats - The Search for Protection*, 58 California Law Review (1970) 1169.

Mello, S, M., *Administering the Antidote to Computer Viruses: A Comment on United States v. Morris*, 19 Rutgers Computer and Technology Law Journal (1993) 259.

Menell, P. S., *An Analysis of the Scope of Copyright Protection*, 41 Stanford Law Review (1989) 1045.

Nimmer, R. T., and Krauthaus, P. A., *Information as Property: Databases and Commercial Property*, 1 International Journal of Law and Information Technology (1993) 3.

Oddi, A. S., *An Uneasier Case for Copyright Than for Patent Protection of Computer Programs*, 72 Nebraska Law Review (1993) 351.

Miller, A., *Copyright Protection for Computer Programs, Databases and Computer-Generated Works; Is Anything New Since CONTU?*, 106 Harvard Law Review (1993) 994.

Plishner, J., *It's None of Your Business - Or Is It? California Addresses the Computer Age*, 8 Rutgers Computer and Technology Law Journal (1981) 235.

Reed, C., *The Liability of Expert System Producers*, 1 Computer Law and Practice (1985) 12.

Riley, T., *Data Protection Today and Some Trends*, 17 Law-Technology (1987) 3.

Rosen, A. H., *Virtual Reality: Copyrightable Subject Matter and the Scope of Judicial Protection*, 33 Jurimetrics Journal (1992) 35.

Rosenbaum, J. I., *The European Commission's Draft Directive on Data Protection*, 33 Jurimetrics Journal (1992) 1.

Rowland, D., *Liability for Defective Software*, 22 Cambrian Law Review (1991) 78.

Samuelson, P., *Some New Kinds of Authorship*, 53 Univ. of Pittsburgh Law Review (1992) 685.

Samuelson, P., *Digital Media and the Changing Face of Intellectual Property Law*, 16 Rutgers Computer & Technology Law Journal (1990) 323.

Samuelson, P., *Liability for Defective Electronic Information*, 36 Communications of the ACM (1993) 21.

Scott, A., *Software as 'Goods': Nullum Simile est Idem*, 3 Computer Law and Practice (1987) 133.

Simitis, S., *Reviewing Privacy in an Information Society*, 135 University of Pennsylvania Law Review (1987) 707.

Simpson, M. J., *999! My Computer's Stopped Breathing*, 10 Computer Law and Security Report (1994) 76.

Staines, A., *Computer Sales: "Caveat Distributor"*, 48 Modern Law Review (1985) 345.

Tapper, C., *Computer Crime: Scotch Mist?*, [1987] Criminal Law Review 4.

Tapper, C., *New European Directions in Data Protection*, 3 Journal of Law and Information Science (1992) 9.

Wasik, M., *Law Reform Proposals on Computer Misuse* [1989] Criminal Law Review. 257.

Wasik, M., *Surveying Computer Crime*, 1 Computer Law and Practice (1985) 110.

Wehlau, A., *Software Protection Under European Community Law*, 2 Law, Computers and Artificial Intelligence (1993) 3.

Wiebe, A., *European Copyright Protection of Software from a German Perspective*, 9 Computer Law and Practice (1993) 79.

Whittaker, S., *European Product Liability and Intellectual Products*, 105 Law Quarterly Review (1989) 125.

Scotland and the Union

HUME PAPERS ON PUBLIC POLICY
Volume 2, No. 2

Edited by Patrick S. Hodge

This book debates the future of the Anglo-Scottish Union of 1707. A team of economists, lawyers, industrialists, historians, journalists and diplomats set out the case for the continuation of the Anglo-Scottish Union of 1707, in whatever form of governmental structure may emerge as the UK move into the twenty-first century. In no way an uncritical apologia for the status quo, this book is a forceful argument that Scotland's problems can only be solved in the wider British, European and general international contexts.

The Hume Papers on Public Policy are available by subscription or individually through bookshops.

Subscription Rates (Quarterly)

Individuals		Instititions	
UK and EC	£34	UK and EC	£68
Overseas	£38	Overseas	£76
N. America	$58	N. America	$116

Back Issues   £10.95/$19.50

Postage: Surface postage is included in the subscription. Please add £10/$18 for airmail delivery.

For further details please contact:
Edinburgh University Press, 22 George Square, Edinburgh EH8 9LF
Tel: 031 650 4689, Fax: 031 662 0053

In Search of New Constitutions

HUME PAPERS ON PUBLIC POLICY
Volume 2, No. 1

Edited by Hector L. MacQueen

A wide-ranging examination of the current state of the

British and French Constitutions following the

ratification of the Treaty of Maastricht, and of the

development of constitutionalism in Russia as far as

Yeltsin's constitutional proposals of late 1993. This book

also considers the place of nationalism in the modern

political order.

The **Hume Papers on Public Policy** are available by subscription or individually through bookshops.

Subscription Rates (Quarterly)

Individuals		Instititions	
UK and EC	£34	UK and EC	£68
Overseas	£38	Overseas	£76
N. America	$58	N. America	$116

Back Issues   £10.95/$19.50

Postage
Surface postage is included in the subscription. Please add £10/$18 for airmail delivery.

For further details please contact:
Edinburgh University Press, 22 George Square, Edinburgh EH8 9LF
Tel: 031 650 4689, Fax: 031 662 0053

HUME PAPERS ON PUBLIC POLICY

•

Recent Issues have been devoted to:

Sex Equality: Law and Economics:

Examines the development and effect of modern
policy and law regarding sex equality, and assessing
the future prospects and desirable directions in both
policy and law.

•

Money Laundering:

Examines the topical and exciting subject of money
laundering. Five leading commentators and
academics tackle the intracacies of international and
European Community aspects of money laundering.

•

Universities, Corporate Governance, Deregulation:

A collection of informative and thought-provoking
essays on the debate about the role of the state and
the nature of self-regulation in the modern world.